AF669070

# EDUCATION: Planning and Human Development

# EDUCATION

## Planning and Human Development

*(In 8 Volumes)*

## Emerging Challenges of Educational Systems

(Volume 7)

V.C. PANDEY

DELHI—110 033

**EDUCATION: Planning and Human Development**
*(Education)*

Rs. 7000 (Set in 8 Vols.)

© V.C. Pandey

ISBN: 81-8205-006-5 (Set)
ISBN: 81-8205-013-8 (Vol. 7)

All rights reserved. No part of this book may be reproduced in any manner without written permission.

Published in 2003 in India by
Isha Books, D-43, Prithviraj Road
Adarsh Nagar, Delhi-110 033

*Lasertypesetting by:* Varsha Graphics, Delhi
*Printed at:* Chawla Offset Press, Delhi

# Preface

The information age presents an interconnected world of knowledge. The new information and communication technologies (ICTs) transformed the concepts of educational system we have followed traditionally. The advent of virtual classrooms and video-desktop technologies promises interesting possibilities of teaching and learning at anyplace, anytime and anywhere. Virtual learning environments represent an entirely new form of educational technology. They offer the educational institutions of the world a complex set of opportunities and challenges.

Today, a shift in education is becoming evident where more responsibility is being placed on the individual for his or her learning, instead of solely on the teacher. Subsequently, the teacher's role is also changing. Teachers themselves also need to be highly technologically literate, needing the competence and confidence to prepare students for a global information society. Education is becoming a lifelong learning and training process, developing transferable skills and knowledge that can be applied to competitive markets where knowledge and information is being traded as a commodity.

Educational institutions around the world are being forced to compete globally, by engaging in entrepreneurial activities to sustain themselves in an uncertain and competitive world. Countries are now realising the economic potential and value of technology in education. As such, it is vital that education systems embrace and implement technology into their schools to produce citizens capable of living in the twenty first century where technology is encroaching more and more into everyday life.

The present book provides a comprehensive analysis of challenges faced by education systems in a digitised and globalised world. It provides an authentic account of elements and processes that need to be considered in this changing context, at all levels of education. Students, teachers, policy makers, researchers and curriculum developers will find it most useful.

***Editor***

# Contents

# 1

# Education: Challenges of Globalisation

Globalisation impacts on many facets of life, including education. Rapid developments in technology and communication are foreseeing changes within school systems across the world as ideas, values and knowledge, vital to education, cross nation states and boundaries. The rise of a global society, driven by technology and communication developments are shaping children, the future citizens of the world into 'global citizens', intelligent people with a broad range of skills and knowledge to apply to a competitive, information based society.

Globalisation is also creating a fast paced, competitive environment through technology and communication which education systems must keep up with. Countries are now realising the economic potential and value of technology in education. The introduction of technology into the classroom is changing the nature of delivering education to students from primary through to tertiary levels. Print literacy, although still widely used is gradually giving way to a new form of electronic literacy "more and more programs and education materials are becoming available in electronic form, more and more teachers are preparing materials in electronic form; and more and more students are generating papers, assignments and projects in electronic form". Blackboards are now being replaced by video projection screens, books with storage device servers and CD ROMs as well as the emergence of on-line digital libraries. Even exams and grades are gradually becoming available through electronic means and notebooks are starting to give way to laptops. Also, students can be examined through computer managed learning systems and do tutorial exercises on a computer rather than in a classroom. Such developments in education portray that there has been a shift from industrialisation to information based societies.

Subsequently, technology is foreseeing a change in the education environment towards a reliance on electronic sources to deliver material. With such changes and the emergence of video conferencing and the internet, the barriers of distance are being broken down at a rapid rate, a key aspect of globalisation. Children and adults can now learn in a variety of ways and no longer have to be physically present at an education institution in order to learn, a definite advantage of flexible delivery systems. It allows for exploration of new areas of learning and thinking.

It is estimated there are over 43 million hosts connected to the internet with access to approximately 320 million pages of information, figures that reflect the potential influence the internet can have on education alone. However, there is little doubt that the development and deployment of information and communication technologies will have enormous implications on access, institutional functioning and the teaching and learning process. Many institutions as direct providers of learning opportunities to students are using technology to deliver its programs, courses and tuition support.

The information technology revolution is foreseeing the development of new kinds of institutions such as 'virtual universities' which are delocalised across cyberspace, institutions with no real buildings and location as such, just web pages providing access to information, knowledge and ideas. The transformation of technology and communications into education systems is being seen as a dawn of an new era where most colleges and universities must decide whether to change a little and remain in the academic candle industry or change a lot and launch themselves into the academic electrical business.

An increase in information technology businesses has been developing and replacing industrialisation since World War II. The rapid growth of television services, with their immense influence as media of mass communication, has been very relevant in the technological shift. Other large contributions to this shift include the transistor and space satellites. The transistor is particularly significant for computers and control engineering whilst the establishment of space satellites has played a dramatic role in telephone and television communication. However the primary advancement made in communication and information based technology over the years is the Internet, which is a massive network of computers located throughout the world. These computers maintain libraries of text, images, computer software, and other forms of data that can be accessed by anyone, anywhere, at any time. However, for this implementation of technology and communication to be successful and to educate a society, both the students and teachers need to be technologically literate. Thus the roles of the teachers and students are changing. The introduction of the internet into classrooms means that students must filter through a mass of information that is available to them and learn to deal with the complexity of this information. The internet is providing students with an interconnected world of knowledge to explore which they must decipher for themselves.

Communication technology is offering new challenges for students of all abilities as they can discuss issues of concern with their fellow students from around the world, thus developing communication and interpersonal skills, fostering a mutual understanding across countries and cultures. Developments in the delivery of education is allowing for individuals to explore new areas of learning and thinking that could not be done with a pen and paper. They are discovering knowledge through inquiry and experimentation rather than memorizing facts in a teacher dominated classroom setting. In fact, students no longer need to be physically present to learn as education material is becoming more and more readily available over the internet, through video conferencing, and tape recordings. Institutions are now turning towards the use of the internet to deliver courses to students at a distance and enhance educational programs delivered on campus with increasing frequency.

The development of flexible delivery programs is being seen as a significant advancement in the delivery of education. However, it has been suggested that those students who can explore the vast resources available to them from the comfort of their home will become increasingly impatient with traditional classroom practice. In contrast it is also believed that universal, unlimited, anywhere, anytime access to powerful telecomputers has helped children of all ages "retain their love for learning, improve academic performance and help prepare them for a world in which self-directed lifelong learning is a survival skill".

Teachers themselves need to be highly technologically literate, needing the competence and confidence to prepare students for a global information society. Teachers are using technology to empower themselves but are now finding themselves in an education system where they are no longer the sole 'fountain of information' but a facilitator and pointer towards information.

In an interconnect world, where technology and communication is delivering the world to students, there must be an education curriculum that is both extensive, international and open to new ideas, values and thoughts. The focus needs to be on skills which can be applied to solving global problems and surviving in an ever changing world of shifting circumstances. Education institutions need to provide students with the skills and knowledge required to be productive citizens in a global environment. A global education should teach about issues that cross national boundaries, and interconnected systems on ecological, cultural, economical, political and technological grounds.

Globalisation and technological advancements are delivering and increasing access to the world and subsequently subjects should reflect this global outlook as we combine knowledge, creativity and intelligence through electronic connection spanning time and distance. Subsequently, there is a demand for graduates who are highly proficient in dealing with the dramatic scientific, technological and cross cultural changes occurring throughout the world.

While technology and communication developments have been presented as beneficial to education environments, the cost of equipping every student and educator with today's technology is staggering, especially when facing increasingly tight constraints placed on education budgets.

However, it can be argued that technology is becoming a lot cheaper when compared to the past, with falling prices making technology educational resources cost competitive with printed materials. Just as technology and communication seems to be creating a divide between the 'haves' and the 'have nots', resulting in a bifurcated society of those who can afford such information technology and those who can't, so too does globalisation. While education institutions in western societies are embracing technology, developing countries are once again left behind, too weak and fragile to implement development programs for education, let alone introduce technology as well. While third world states encourage their citizens to seek more education, severe limitations in delivering basic services are a problem.

A lack of infrastructure and funding makes it difficult to implement any technological and communication advancements into systems that require substantial financial resources where a majority of technology and resources must go to disease prevention and health care. However, despite differences in economy, polity, culture and society, second and third worlds have adopted educational ideals from western thought and are anxious to appear modern and therefore promote education as a symbol of modernity and development to their own population and the foreign countries.

Technology and communication systems will continue to develop and encroach on educational systems worldwide. Globalisation will further drive these changes, presenting new options and challenges to both students and teachers and revolutionize the delivery of education. However, as the world becomes further and further bifurcated it will be a challenge for education systems to keep up with the development and economic implications of technology, and in particular for developing and third worlds to introduce technology and communication systems into their education infrastructure. However any changes in education through technology and communication will also impact on its delivery and thus have an effect on the receiving culture.

Globalisation is a process which has affected many areas of life, one of those being education. In the twentieth century, many developing countries have experienced a growth in the educational facilities available to them due to an influx of institutions from the West. This has raised concerns as to the effect such spreading of education will have on the cultures of the receiving countries. Some believe that this process is an invaluable opportunity for the people of the developing countries to raise their skills and standards of education.

Others fear that it is merely a modern version of cultural imperialism that will lead to the creation of a universal, ultimately Western society. From as early as the mid-nineteenth century western countries have been expanding their educational institutions across foreign borders. The current university institutions in the Indian sub-continent have their origins from the colonial powers. So the current spread of education across international borders is not a new phenomenon. However it is recently that the issue has been raised, as to the effect of this internationalisation of education on cultures.

There are two main sides to the argument one side claims that education which moves from Western countries into developing ones is tailored to the needs of the specific culture receiving it. The other argues that as a result of the globalisation of education, cultures are being taken over by the West in a process of cultural imperialism designed to create a global, essentially Western culture. To begin with I will look at the former argument then follow with a discussion about the latter.

One aspect of the globalisation of education has been the creation of 'twinning projects' between one Western and one non-Western university. This results in the creation of a course which is mutually agreed upon and which both institutions can gain from. The main content of the course is the same but each institution can adapt the material to local needs, resulting in a programme containing an international perspective and local concerns. Such programs do not force the values and beliefs of one culture onto another, but allow both countries to enhance their educational materials whilst ensuring that their culture is nurtured and maintained.

Global educators are insensitively spreading their own views of the world onto developing nations in the mistaken belief that they are actually helping people. Such views would imply that the spread of higher education is doing more harm than good because although these people are receiving an education, they are doing so at the cost of their unique culture.

The spread of education internationally, as a result of globalisation, has clearly had effects on cultures world wide. However, this is not the only change that can been seen. The capitalist society is gradually becoming global with a strong emphasis on free-trade emerging. Educational institutions have reacted accordingly, by becoming more market oriented, focussing their energy more on creating funds rather than providing sufficient education for students.

The main trade policy developments since the early and mid 1980s have led to greater market orientation and freer trade, under the leadership of the World Trade Organisation, since 1994. The World Trade Organisation is a forum for harmonising trade conditions around the world. All the members of the World Trade Organisation are committed to all the Multilateral Trade Agreements. In regards to freer trade, in both developed and developing countries tariffs have been significantly reduced, since the establishment of GATT, and more are to be reduced in the near future under the World Trade Agreement. Services trade, such as education, has also been brought into the multilateral system. Many countries are, as with goods, opening their markets for services trade and investment either unilaterally or through regional or multilateral negotiations.

The underlying philosophy of free trade in international trade agreements (such as the World Trade Agreement) is that, whenever something can be provided by the private sector, conditions should exist so this can occur. Thus, government actions, which obstruct the growth of the private sector, should be identified and destroyed. Because of this 'increasingly dominant neo-liberal environment...universities in the industrialised states were drawn closer to the corporate world.'

As well as the World Trade Organisation being established in 1994, at the last round of GATT, the General Agreement on Trade and Services (GATS) was also established. This was the first multilateral agreement on services, as a comprehensive agreement on international trade and services, including education. Traditionally, trade agreements had been almost solely about reducing tariffs and other trade barriers. It is an extension of the General Agreement on Tariffs and Trade to services, through GATS.

The GATS general framework is for no discrimination in favour of national providers. This has been seen in Australia in many sectors, including banking and communication, but now is also evident in education. For example, in the 1999-2000 Australian budget there was a major reform of non-government school funding.

Under the rules of GATS 'transparency and progressive liberalism' of services applies to all member countries. There are a number of GATS specific rules. These include: slight provisions for restrictions on monopolies by the particular government; 'uniform trade policies', that is, consistent trade policies in regards to services throughout the member countries;

acknowledgment of foreign professional qualifications; and a reduction in misrepresented subsidies and the like. All of these rules undoubtedly fall under the banner of further liberalisation in regards to services, such as education.

Additionally, GATS is administered by the Council for Trade and Services, which is notified annually of changes in national laws in regards to services such as education. Other member countries are also able to complain to the council about other member's regulations. Thus, there is quite a lot of pressure on member countries of the WTO to conform to this increasing liberalisation of services, such as education. However, the GATS framework also allows nations to have an individual choice as to what extent services, such as education, are fully open to free trade. Thus, although so far Australia has committed itself to some aspects of free trade in education, it is not yet significantly threatening to public education.

Shortly before the 1999 December Seattle World Trade Organisation meeting the US Trade Ambassador, Charlene Barshefsky announced that the US specifically wanted free trade in education incorporated in the new round of negotiations. Her justifications were purely economic - because much more is achievable in an open market. Thus, this is another example of the recent strong push towards an increasing global and liberalised education system around the world. Both the WTO and one of the leaders in the world economic sphere, the US, are pushing in that direction. There are many elements currently present that indicate that education is already emeshed in the world's free trade and competitive philosophy.

Firstly, there is cross border supply. This is where the provider of education and the buyer do not move, for example, delivering education across the world through satellite broadcasting.

Secondly, in regards to consumption abroad, there is a commercial presence of foreign investors in many host countries. For example, foreign universities are setting up courses or institutions in other countries.

Thirdly, there is commercial presence, that is, where the provider establishes a physical presence in the host country.

Lastly, there is the presence of persons who leave their country to study or provide education abroad. For example, academics on short-term contracts and international students in Australia. However, there are still some barriers to these four modes of delivery in regards to the globalisation of education present. For example, there are national requirements to set up an institution or courses and to receive government grants.

Additionally, there are government monopolies. Moreover, there are direct restrictions on students, for example, immigration and visa requirements. However, if the new round of negotiations at the World Trade Organisation succeeds in eliminating the barriers to complete free trade in education, the 'private sector will receive enormous power to undermine the public delivery of education services'.

Thus education has been effected by the globalisation of the world economy, especially in regards to free trade and privitisation to a moderate extent, but there is much more potential for it to develop even more in the near future.

## Internationalisation of Education

In an era typified by the globalisation of technology, communications, and the integration of worldwide capital and labour markets, educators are being forced to respond to a new set of challenges. The Internationalisation of education can be given many definitions. It can be described as integration of culture into teaching methods or processes by which education becomes more internationally orientated. However perhaps a better description is the process that prepares the community for successful participation in an increasingly interdependent world, fosters global understanding and develops skills for effective living, working in a diverse world.

Universities and colleges around the world are increasingly becoming forced to compete in the global capitalist market and engage in entrepreneurial activity to sustain themselves in an increasingly ' uncertain world '. Universities are no longer always state controlled and are, more often than not, controlled by transnational companies carrying names like Microsoft Corporation.

Government's support universities that market themselves internationally as it provides education locally whilst at the same time creating revenue. Education, in this sense, has literally become ' commodified'. But, is this commodity accessible to all, including people in developing countries? Is the structure of education changing to survive on the ' open market '? The internationalisation of higher education can be linked to various internal and external changes in the international system. Externally, there have been changes in the labour market, which have resulted in calls for more knowledged and skilled workers, and workers with deeper understandings of languages, cultures and business methods from all over the world.

Modern education is almost exclusively focused on preparing children for an urban future, as consumers in a global free market. Due to this internationalisation, educational institutions are being encouraged by governing authorities and transnational corporations to ' market themselves overseas. Internationalising education means courses and topics, either existing or new, must be delivered in a global capacity which naturally means via the Internet and online. Coping with this technology requires huge amounts of time and money, not to mention expertise and skilled workers to deal with the technology.

Tragically, Government funding to universities is suffering massive cutbacks leaving many long-standing institutions with little money, yet they are still expected to compete ' globally '. In order to attract foreign students and therefore foreign revenue, universities must provide the global consumer with what is demanded. Courses must be flexible, adaptable, online and above all, interactive between the various cultures around the world.

For universities, the internationalisation of education doesn't come easily. The internationalisation of education almost gives the impression that the educational institution is no longer in control. In order to survive, universities rely on the business of domestic and foreign students. These students in turn make their decision on which institution to attend by the way their courses are marketed. Unbeknown to the prospective students, universities face many problems in the new race to become a successful competitor on the global market.

Modern education is focused almost entirely on continuing the processes of globalisation, where " the graduates of tomorrow will be trained, above all, to keep the wheels of the global economy turning, with all the implications that has for nature and society." To get down to the business of education, it is hardly surprising that since modern and 'internationalised' education produces urban consumers, that business is taking interest in how educational institutions are being run. Corporate interests are reshaping education in accordance with it's own profit chasing interests.

The 'internationalisation' of education is carrying the "full ensemble of western institutions to much of the developing world. Together with this and the decline of international economic aid, there has been a considerable amount of underpinning for university development in the poorer countries.

The role of education has become more linked to globally competitive positions. Subsequent changes in university functions have lead universities toward" direct entrepreneurial activity to sustain themselves." This in turn produces a change in institutional approaches to the development of overseas education. University courses must now be cross-cultural in content, which is in association with the growing number of students, particularly in the 1990's, searching for higher education outside of their own country. It is estimated that "by the year 2025, the world's post secondary institutions will be expected to accommodate some 200 million students." This is compared to 82 million in 1995. It is also a fact that domestic and foreign full-fee paying students will make up the majority of this predicted number. The World Declaration for Higher Education for the Twenty-

First Century has reflected a commitment to provide "access to higher education...based on the merit of the individual."

Access to higher education is a right, it should not be limited to ' the better off ' due to inability to pay. Education is becoming more invaluable to individuals as society changes to cope in a globalising world. In today's environment, education provides individuals with a better chance of employment, which in turn leads to a better lifestyle, power and status.

In an internationalised society, globalisation of education depends upon the existence of classes able to pay. Education, particularly full-fee education is an expensive commodity, those who receive it are regarded as being better off'. The internationalisation of education leads to the distribution of future status and power. Western institutions conveying their interests overseas by marketing ' our ' universities is rather like " selling a standard product that is marketed as being the right product for all occasions." The need to sell education overseas is increasingly being interpreted as " a lifeline for higher education and vocational training providers squeezed by shrinking government education budgets ". Universally, higher education has become an extremely competitive enterprise on the global capitalist market.

Globalisation has had many obvious effects on education. As globalisation progresses, we will continue to see many changes in the structure and content of the education system internationally. Technology and communication systems change the way education is delivered as well as roles played by both teachers and students. The development of this technology is facilitating the transition from an industrial based society to an information based one. The delivery of education has become more of a global process thus raising questions as to the effects on cultures world wide. There has been suggestions that the globalisation of education is a new form of western cultural imperialism.

As a result of world moves toward free trade, the commodification' of education has emerged , thus rendering educational institutions as profit making enterprises. This has led to international concerns about the affordability and accessibility of the commodity. Globalisation has transformed education and will continue to do so, leaving us with a future that is more unpredictable than ever.

The demands of globalization increase pressures on the education system form groups with the greatest political power, increasing inequality and segregation in schools. They increase violence, instability, and political conflict, which acts negatively on the education system. It produces the removal of teachers and students , instability in the financing of education, and difficulties in adopting a long-range perspective in the management of educatio. The most frequently-used device is certainly that of the "elective affinity effects" between globalization, neo-liberal ideas, and certain correspondence effects, correlation, proximity, similarity, relationship, parallelism, or harmony produced in the education system such as: educational productionism, deterioration of working conditions for teachers, privatization, assessment pressures, international comparisons of performance, decentralization, etc. For example,

Even one of the most important education reforms associated with globalization - decentralization in the management and financing of education - seems to have little or no impact on the delivery of education within the classroom the form in which such delivery is made in the classroom is an important aspect of the production of knowledge, and that classrooms appear to be basically untouched. But that is only one part of the process of the production of knowledge and, moreover. The question is whether it wouldn't be possible to offer a better-fitting interpretation of the effects of globalization on education. To do so, instead looking at it as a background cause that operates through "elective affinities", it should be treated as a part of the environment within which education develops, affecting relevant dimensions of the contexts within which it operates and to which it must respond and adopt.

There are five context dimensions within which the on-going transformations are important and, consequently, represent challenges for education in the 21 century. They are access to information; storehouse of knowledge; labor market; availability of ICTs for education; and divesrse worlds of life.

— *Access to Information*: Throughout history, information has been scarce and difficult to access. Ever since the invention of writing, the richest information has been found in texts which were only accessible to a small minority even up to the 19th century, during which illiteracy levels were still extraordinarily high throughout the world. The invention of the printing press produced a veritable revolution by making the writing within texts easy to reproduce. Still, it was some time before books and magazines were available to the masses, and only in the last few decades have we seen a real explosion. Today, the situation of available and accessible information is completely different. It is increasingly more abundant and easy to obtain, as witnessed by the internet and www. The people who access the internet, who still represent a minority in the world, are highly concentrated in northern countries. This number is steadily growing. It is estimated that the number will reach 1 billion within the next 10 years. The problem for education currently is not where to find information, but how to offer access without excluding , and how to teach, learn, select, assess, interpret, classify, and use the information. There is an additional question involved here: how to develop the "higher cognitive functions of "problem-solving, problem-finding, planning, reflecting, creativity, deeper understanding" -that are indispensable within a medium saturated with information, and avoiding that education be reduced to the level of basic or elementary skills.

— *Storehouse of knowledge*: Transmitted and acquired knowledge constitutes an essential dimension of the entire educational process. Not long ago, this function of inculcation of knowledge was favored by the fact that the global platform of knowledge, and the bases of disciplinary knowledge, were relatively small and stable. This facilitated the task of schools. Today, on the other hand, knowledge increases and changes very rapidly.

— *Labour market*: Throughout history, education has fulfilled the function of preparing people for exercising adult roles; particularly for entering the labor market. It is often argued today that globalization has carried this to a perverse extreme, placing upon education a utilitarian, business-oriented function that is no more than the mere training of the labor force. Be that as it may, it is evident that education here faces an accelerated change in context. Increasing numbers of people are employed in a service sector in which one of the entrance requirements is to have acquired necessary inter-personal skills. Certain occupations demand increasingly higher levels of schooling and reward increasing levels accordingly, and thus increasing the distance between those who have less and those who have more schooling. In general, a growing number of jobs require that people know how to read and understand technical information. The same is the case for the requirement to be computer-literate. Moreover, people now need to be trained for unstable career paths and to expect not only probable changes of employers, but changes in occupation and economic sector as well. In a deeper sense, we raise a question here of a structural nature in terms of future relations between education and labor.

— *Availability of ICTs for education*: The technological context within which education has unfolded has been highly stable throughout time- more so than the contexts of information and knowledge. After the invention of printing, schools adjusted technologically to broadcasting of lectures, texts, pencils, and to chalk and blackboard. Only late in time did they add the overhead projector and, later, the TV and VCR. But all of this has begun to change rapidly and deeply with the global spread of NICT. One of the major constants of school life - the isolation of schools - has begun to diminish through the connection of schools to networks; just as one of the constituent principals of learning begins to be replaced by hypertext. The learning technologies represented go from the analog to the digital, from broadcasts to interactive forms, and from exogenous control of processes (away from the student) to autonomous control (by the student). TV represents the medium "in which all intelligence finds its point of origin" of transmission; in this case, the teacher. Video tapes represent a step forward, but permit greater control on the part of the user (when and where to reproduce them). Books may be taken from one place to the other, and texts read in the order that one desires.

Face-to-face classes can have a larger interactive component. But the leap occurred, according to Tapscott, recently with the advent of "digital media", starting with the most rudimentary types of computer-aided instruction: routines, pre-programmed tutorials, and teaching games, all of which permit a greater degree of self-control of the process on the part of the student, and various interactive forms. The latter have increased with the use of hyper-media -which employ a combination of media - being able to result in on-line forums, MUDs (multi-user domain), which are sites on the Net where users create and participate, in real time, in a virtual situation.

— *Divesrse worlds of life*: Education should take into account changes taking place in the immediate cultural context within which it develops; that is, within the context of feelings and meanings that permit it to function in a stable manner in regard to its own participants - students and teachers - and to families and the community. There is a "socialization deficit" within contemporary society that he attributes to a crisis in the function of cultural uniformization of the nation - a classic State and school function - and to the loss in the educability of traditional agents - families, schools, and, we might add, of churches and local communities. There has especially been a decline in the role of the teacher as socializing agent, along with the appearance of new competing modes of socialization, such as television, for example. This socialization deficit does not only have to do with transformations and weaknesses of socialization agents; rather, in a deeper sense, it has to do with the problem of the weakening of the foundations upon which we define social and personal identities and, on the other, the loss of ideals, the absence of utopias, the lack of meaning.

## Globalisation: Challenges to Higher Education

Today, as a result of globlaisation we are facing significant new trends in the gloal environment that affect the shape and mode and the purpose of education systems. Knowledge accumulation and application have become major factors in economic development and are increasingly at the core of a country's competitive advantage in the global economy. The combination of increased computing power, diminishing prices of hardware and software, improvement of wireless and satellite technologies, and reduced telecommunication costs has all but removed the space and time barriers to information access and exchange.

The role of higher education in the construction of knowledge economies and democratic societies is more influential than ever. Indeed, higher education is central to the creation of the intellectual capacity on which knowledge production and utilization depend and to the promotion of the lifelong-learning practices necessary to update individual knowledge and skills. Another favorable development is the emergence of new types of higher institutions and new forms of competition, inducing traditional institutions to change their modes of operation and delivery and to take advantage of the opportunities offered by the new information and communication technologies.

However this technological transformation carries the real danger of a growing digital divide between and within nations. Even as these new opportunities and challenges emerge, most developing and transition countries continue to wrestle with difficulties stemming from inadequate responses to long-standing problems facing their higher education systems. Among these unresolved challenges are the need to expand higher education coverage in a sustainable way, inequalities of access and outcomes, problems of educational quality and relevance, and rigid governance structures and management practices.

Higher education institutions are unique in their ability to integrate and create synergy among these three dimensions. Sustainable transformation and growth throughout the economy are not possible without the capacity-building contribution of an innovative higher education system. This is especially true in low-income countries with weak institutional capacity and limited human capital.

Higher education supports the opportunity and empowerment dimensions. Access to higher education can open better employment and income opportunities to underprivileged students, thereby decreasing inequity. The norms, values, attitudes, ethics, and knowledge that higher institutions can impart to students constitute the social capital necessary to construct healthy civil societies and socially cohesive cultures. It is doubtful that any developing country could make significant progress toward achieving the United Nations Millennium Develoment Goals (MDGs) for education-universal enrollment in primary education and elimination of gender disparities in primary and secondary education-without a strong higher education system.

Higher education supports the rest of the education system through the training of teachers and school principals, the involvement of specialists from higher education institutions in curriculum design and educational research, and the establishment of admission criteria that influence the content and methods of teaching and learning at the secondary level. A similar argument applies to the contribution of postsecondary medical education, especially the training of medical doctors, epidemiologists, public health specialists, and hospital managers, to meeting the basic health MDGs.

Research on the dynamics of knowledge-driven development has identified the converging roles of four contributing factors: a country's macroeconomic incentive and institutional regime, its ICT infrastructure, its national innovation system, and the quality of its human resources. Of these, the contribution of higher education is vital with respect to the national innovation system and the development of human resources. In this context, continued government support of higher education is justified by three important considerations:

the existence of externalities from higher education, equity issues, and the supportive role of higher education in the education system as a whole.

Investments in higher education generate major external benefits that are crucial for knowledge-driven economic and social development. Private investment in higher education can be suboptimal because individuals do not capture all the benefits of education. Afew examples will illustrate how education yields benefits to society as a whole. Technological innovations and the diffusion of scientific and technical innovations lead to higher productivity, and most of these innovations are the products of basic and applied research undertaken in universities. Progress in the agriculture, health, and environment sectors, in particular, is heavily dependent on the application of such innovations.

Higher education facilitates nation building by promoting greater social cohesion, trust in social institutions, democratic participation and open debate, and appreciation of diversity in gender, ethnicity, religion, and social class. Furthermore, pluralistic and democratic societies depend on research and analysis that are fostered through social sciences and humanities programs. Improved health behaviors and outcomes also yield strong social benefits, and higher education is indispensable for training the needed health care professionals.

Imperfections in capital markets limit the ability of individuals to borrow sufficiently for higher education, thereby hindering the participation of meritorious but economically disadvantaged groups. Although more than 60 countries have student loan programs, access to affordable loans frequently remains restricted to a minority of students. Moreover, these loans are not necessarily available to the students with limited resources who most need financial aid. Very few countries have national programs reaching more than 10 percent of the student population, and these exceptions are rich countries such as Australia, Canada, Sweden, the United Kingdom, and the United States. In addition, where they do exist, student loans are not always available for the whole range of academic programs and disciplines.

Higher education plays a key role in supporting basic and secondary education, thereby buttressing the economic externalities produced by these lower levels. Improved higher education is necessary for sustainable progress in basic education. The supply of qualified teachers and school leaders, capacity for curriculum design, research on teaching and learning, economic analysis and management-these and many more components of basic education reform are hampered by weak higher education systems. A comprehensive approach to the development of the education sector is required, along with a balanced distribution of budgetary resources to ensure that countries invest appropriately in higher education, with attention to their progress toward the Millennium Development Goals.

While many undergraduate and professional education programs can be offered in separate institutions (business and law are examples), high-cost activities such as basic research and various types of specialized graduate training are more efficiently organized in combination with undergraduate training. Cross-subsidization across educational disciplines, programs, and levels leads to public-good effects that are valuable but are difficult to quantify. In addition, there are economies of scale that justify public support of expensive programs such as basic sciences that are almost natural monopolies. Notwithstanding the methodological difficulties involved in measuring externalities, the existence of these important public benefits indicates that the costs of insufficient investment in higher education can be very high. These costs can include reduced ability of a country to compete effectively in global and regional economies; a widening of economic and social disparities; declines in the quality of life, in health status, and in life expectancy; an increase in unavoidable public expenditures on social welfare programs; and a deterioration of social cohesion.

Sustainable transformation and growth throughout the economy cannot be achieved without an innovative higher education system to help build the absorptive capacity that is required if private sector investment and donor resources are to have a lasting productive impact. At the same time, the development of a holistic education system calls for a comprehensive approach to resource allocation. Certain guidelines can be applied to ensure a balanced distribution of budgetary resources and an appropriate sequencing of investment across the three education subsectors in relation to a country's level of education development, pattern of economic growth, and fiscal situation. Based on the experience of industrial countries that have emphasized the role of education in supporting economic growth and social cohesion, it would seem that an appropriate range for the overall level of investment in education as a share of gross domestic product (GDP) would be between 4 and 6 percent. In this context, expenditures on higher education would generally represent between 15 and 20 percent of all expenditures on public education.

Developing countries that devote more than 20 percent of their education budget to higher education, especially those that have not attained universal primary education coverage, are likely to have a distorted allocation that favors an elitist university system and does not adequately support basic and secondary education. Similarly, countries that spend more than 20 percent of their higher education budget on noneducational expenditures such as student subsidies are likely to be underinvesting in materials, equipment, library resources, and other inputs that are crucial for quality learning.

As their direct involvement in the funding and provision of higher education diminishes, governments rely less on the traditional state control model to make reforms happen. Instead they promote change by guiding and encouraging higher education institutions through a coherent policy framework, an enabling regulatory environment, and appropriate financial incentives.

Countries and higher education institutions willing to take advantage of the new opportunities presented by the knowledge economy and the ICT revolution must be proactive in fostering innovations and launching meaningful reforms in a coherent policy framework. Although there is no blueprint that is valid for all countries, a common prerequisite seems to be a clear vision for the long-term development of a comprehensive, diversified, and well-articulated higher education system. Student mobility can be encouraged by developing open systems that offer recognition of relevant prior experience, degree equivalencies, credit transfer, tuition exchange schemes, access to national scholarships and student loans, and a comprehensive qualifications and lifelong-learning framework.

— The regulatory environment should be one that encourages rather than stifles innovations in public institutions and initiatives by the private sector to expand access to good-quality higher education. Rules for the establishment of new institutions, including private and virtual ones, should be restricted to outlining minimum quality requirements and should not constitute barriers to entry. Other regulatory considerations should be the development of quality assurance mechanisms (evaluation, accreditation, national examinations, rankings, and publication of information), financial controls to which public institutions are required to conform, and intellectual property rights legislation.

— Although public funding remains the main source of support for higher education in most countries, it is being channeled in new ways and is being increasingly supplemented by nonpublic resources. Both of these changes bring market forces to bear in ways heretofore uncommon in the financing of public institutions. New financing strategies have been put in place in the public sector to generate revenue from institutional assets, to mobilize additional resources from students and their families, and to encourage donations from thirdparty contributors. Many governments have also encouraged the creation of private institutions as an effective approach for easing pressures on the public purse and satisfying pent-up demand.

Globalization and the growth of borderless education

raise important issues that affect higher education in all countries but are often beyond the control of any one national government. Among these challenges are new forms of human capital flight that result in a loss of local capacity in fields critical to development; the absence of a proper international accreditation and qualifications framework; the absence of accepted legislation regarding foreign higher education providers; the lack of clear intellectual property regulations governing distance education programs; and barriers to access to information and communication technologies, including the Internet.

Higher education has become a multi-billion dollar market as the quantity of education is increasing rapidly and double every five years. The export of higher education service has contributed significantly to the economy of the US. In 1999 it is estimated that the US, being the largest provider of education services, earned $8,5 billion of the $30 billion market, from this trade alone. The share for Asia is estimated at $10 billion. Higher education has in the past contributed to development by providing national economies with the necessary human resources but criticized for not dealing directly with poverty reduction issues.

Higher education role has shifted more to supporting an economy that is knowledge intensive at a global level. The relevance of higher education systems at local level needs to be rethought in the framework of their relevance in the global context, hence the question as to whether they are still relevant to development at a local level. The issue is of concern as the public good of systems of higher education operating at a global level is debatable. There is a renewal of higher education systems of education in countries of the South and a renewed interest by the donor agencies operating in Africa to support higher education. At national levels new reform policies are being developed and at institutional levels new leadership has embarked on the processes to revive their institutions and write new strategic development plans. International agencies such as the World Bank have also revised their policies towards supporting higher education and have come to accept the view that there is need for investment at all levels of education as a strategy for promoting development. Changes taking place have put a lot of emphasis on the need for accountability to society beyond financial accountability, demand for intellectual leadership, and partnership that could contribute to development.

One of the key features of globalization is increased competition. Competition has become a driving force for innovation and entrepreneurship. Competition in higher education has increased and has become unfair. Countries of the North with their competitive advantage compete with countries from the South for best students, faculty, administrators, and researchers. As a result the intellectual resource from the South are been drained in the process. Sources of high-level skilled labor for the thriving global economy have been mainly the developing countries and Russia during its transition to a capitalist economy.

Competition has resulted in student losses to private for profit higher education, loss of jobs, and in some cases the threat of closure of institutions. Competition in academia has continued to perpetuate the negative effect of globalization such as increasing inequality both between academics within institutions and between academics in different institutions and countries. Trade piracy within a globalizing context and in general has become a problem too for many countries and costs countries a lot in losses despite the adoption of tough laws by organizations such as the World Trade Organization.

International companies and institutions are flooding developing countries with cheap products. In higher education trade, inferior programs that are costly are offered to students in countries of the South especially in countries where there are no quality control mechanisms in place. Even in situations where there are some control measures in place there are institutions that manage to slip through control measures and students are ripped off. The situation has become problematic and some countries find it difficult to protect what they value in education in the same way that countries in the North do. South Africa responded by declaring a moratorium on new partnerships in distance education during a period of transformation whilst putting in place quality control mechanisms. To promote co-operation within a competitive environment there is need to consider current institutional responses to global changes and perceived threat posed by increased competition. Universities in the South have responded differently to the challenges they face under globalisation.

National responses to globalization vary from innovations driven by the need for survival to increased competition and becoming more entrepreneurial. Institutions mainly in Europe have opted to become more entrepreneurial 13 and the newly appointed president at New York University has been pushing an agenda for an enterprise university. The newly formed European

Consortia of Innovative Universities (ECIU) is another example and the emerging literature on entrepreneur universities. There are countries that have embraced the changes and some developing countries have even signed for participation in the General Agreement on Trade in Service (GATS). Hong Kong for example has opted to embrace the changes taking place and capitalize on the opportunities offered to increase access to higher education. Countries that have been unable to increase participation rates due to financial constraints have also opted for opening up their countries for global foreign providers as a cheaper option than investing in the needed infrastructure.

In higher education opportunities for cooperation are created by the emergence of multiple, networked, global knowledge production sites as higher education increasingly looses the monopoly for knowledge production. Two challenges arise for universities in the South. The first is a challenge of becoming part of the networks and the second is the challenge of producing knowledge or using knowledge for development purposes. With the latter, institutions are finding themselves paying more attention to meeting the need for increasing access at the expense of research. Faculty teaching loads have been increasing - leaving little room for research, as survival has become more dependent on fee paying students. Universities from the North have generally responded to globalization by establishing partnerships with other knowledge producers and participation in innovation hubs. Universities in the South need to be part of the new arrangements being forged in the North in knowledge production, dissemination and reconfiguration for production.

Emerging social relations so far largely exclude universities from the South. There is need to include universities of the South in the new trans-institutional arrangements for the development of knowledge production sites and multiple agencies involved in the production and dissemination of knowledge.

Universities from the South have already been indirectly affected by the new market operations in the new information production and dissemination strategies. The universities from the North have recruited the best students, faculty, and researchers from their counterparts in the South. Some institutions, for example, in South Africa have also lost their best senior administrators to the countries in the North and their best students to the institutions that had the best facilities provided by the former discriminatory government. There is need to cooperate in capacity building for those institutions that in some cases have paid little or no attention to knowledge production due to financial constraints.

Partnership between universities could contribute to capacity building in knowledge production and use of knowledge, in delivering and disseminating knowledge to masses of students, in contributing to the development of human resources with high-level skills that in turn could contribute to development. Universities in the South need to take the initiative in strengthening themselves to be able to respond to the needs of a new global economy.

An example of a model geared toward enabling universities to take the initiative in their revival is that presented by the Foundation Partnership for "Strengthening African Universities". The partnership has decided to provide support to institutions in Africa that are responding to new challenges posed by globalisation and the need to respond to changing societal needs. The support is provided in the form of grants to institutions to develop and implement strategic plans, support for research on change in African universities, support to university leadership to participate in global networks and professional associations, and promoting debates on change and the role of universities for development. The foundations provide support over an extended period whilst institutions work on mechanisms for sustainability. Private and public sector cooperation could contribute to development. Higher education systems of some developing countries have largely remained elite despite the recognition of the importance of increasing participation rates.

The increasing demand for higher education has not been met mainly due to budgetary constraints. The private sector has a role to play in providing higher education programs to the majority of people who in the past could not access higher education. There could be private-public sector co-operation in this area, for example, to use franchise material from the private sector by the public sector, institutions contracting the private sector companies to deliver instruction in their areas of specialty. One successful story is that of the partnership arrangement between a private company and university in South Africa for first year literacy classes to all students. There is need to encourage and support South to South linkages similar to those promoted through Luced-I &UA for involving higher education institutions directly in development issues. The consortia aims at developing human resources through student, faculty, and researcher exchanges, curriculum development, improved teaching methods, research networking, and joint projects in teaching and research.

Historically the relations between the North and South economically and politically have been underpinned by a pretense to help developing countries improve their economic situation but resulted in those countries getting poorer. Part of the solution is to let those who need help take ownership of development strategies, revise policies, change economic relationships between the rich and the poor, encourage investment in poor countries. There is need for genuine commitment to development and mutually beneficial partnership arrangements between institutions in the North and those in the South. There is need at a global level for the development of policies that are enabling for institutions to access technology and information. If such policies are put in place then universities could participate and play their role in development. There is need to rethink the role of higher education in development because it has become part of the enrichment agenda through agencies such as the WTO and GATS arrangements and not part of the development agenda for sustainable development.

The General Agreement on Trades in Service (GATS), plus other regional trade agreements, are testimony to the increased emphasis on trade and the market economy in this era of globalization. GATS is the first legal trade agreement which focuses exclusively on trade of services - as opposed to trade of products. It is administered by the World Trade Organization, a powerful organization with 144 member countries.

Education is one of the 12 service sectors covered by GATS. The purpose of GATS is to progressively and systematically promote freer trade in services by removing many of the existing barriers to trade. What does this mean for higher education? The current debate on the impact of GATS on higher education is divided, if not polarized. Critics focus on the threat to the role of government, the 'public good' and the quality of education. Supporters highlight the benefits that more trade can bring in terms of innovations through new providers and delivery modes, greater student access and increased economic gain. Trade liberalization has the potential to profoundly change the nature and provision of higher education provision and the role that government plays in that provision. The purpose of this chapter is to discuss both risks and opportunities that GATS brings to higher education and to identify some of the policy implications and issues which need further analysis.

# 2

# Challenges of Higher Education

Innovation is complex and challenging within large organisations such as universities that are part of a mass system of higher education. During the past fifteen years a considerable amount of money has been invested in promoting the use of ICT in higher education, through initiatives such as the teaching and learning technology projects and the computers in education initiatives.

The most successful kind of ICT used in higher education institutions today is electronic mail and it was available in many universities for over a decade before it came into widespread use. Innovations are always most successful when they have an obvious, practical value; in the case of electronic mail, enabling effective communication within one's own organisation or to anywhere in the world at very low cost.

All innovations involve winning people over to change the way they do things and this can never be achieved without adequate and appropriate professional development. Despite the crucial importance of professional development, the top priority must be access to essential technology and equipment. It is these last two factors that have delayed the widespread use of electronic mail for ten years; in many higher education institutions the facilities for email were not available, and in those where they were there was insufficient will and/ or resources to enable individuals to explore its use and understand its benefits.

Today, higher education is going through a maelstrom of change and this in turn is putting pressure on those who work in the system. In market terms, these are pressures to improve productivity. Widening access means that the character and needs of the student population are changing; there are increased numbers without any additional resources, leading to larger classes and increased assessment loads; there is pressure to provide more vocational courses that equip future employees with a wider, less 'academic' range of knowledge and skills.

In short, higher education is subject to economic imperatives defined by government and employers. Of course, it is essential to have a system that provides value for money. Generally the governments cannot afford to develop a mass higher education systemwithout reducing the unit of cost per student. But huge increases in student numbers are not easy to manage and all kinds of other linked changes are causing new problems, e.g. semesterisation which has doubled the assessment load by dividing the academic year into two independent parts; and modularisation which has done away with coherent course groups, making it often impossible to establish any depth of rapport between teacher and students, or between student and student. These things make up a higher education system which is stressful for those who work in it, and it is important to remember that this is the context in which ICT is being introduced.

The dream of policymakers and politicians is that ICT is the answer to the problem of how to create a mass higher education system that is affordable within the national budget. The hope is that ICT will deliver more costeffective teaching and learning. As a result, the introduction of ICT into higher education has been strongly politicised. There are huge expectations without due regard to the difficulties that are an inevitable part of any technological innovation in education. An example of this political euphoria was the announcement in 1996 that £33 million had been awarded by the Millennium Fund, to establish a multisite University of the Highlands and Islands, using ICT as a main medium of teaching. There is no doubt that this is a visionary idea, aimed at providing higher education in their home location to students in extreme rural areas, widely separated from their teachers by moors, mountains and lochs. It is a visionary idea, but it will also involve enormous complexity in establishing both the ICT networking and the changes in work practices essential for collaboration and sharing between many, many individuals in a large number of institutions.

In order to understand the impact upon staff of these changes in the context of higher education, it is useful to look at some of the typologies of institutional management that have emerged from research. For instance, as you read you may like to consider whether you are working in a bureaucratic or a collegial institution. To decide on the answer, you would need to consider factors such as the extent to which your institution is one in which decisions are made by a small management team and implemented by passing requirements down to more junior colleagues through a line management hierarchy.

Or the extent to which it is one in which decisions are made by committees that share power democratically among colleagues, through a process whereby colleagues meet in a forum for open and free debate and, through negotiation, reach a democratic decision. Of course, few if any will recognise the latter as being the way that their institution works. The socalled collegial organisational type is more likely to be one of 'restricted collegiality' , where certain professors exercise enormous power in these apparently democratic committee fora and lobbying prior to the meeting is crucially important. However, the patronage of an institution organised on the basis of 'restricted' or 'contrived' collegiality has certain advantages.

The impact on individuals of externally imposed change is mediated by institutional culture. The experience of the ICT innovation differs widely between one institution and another. One factor in this is that differing values of institutions create different kinds of power structures. For example, the ICT innovation creates career opportunities for the 'early adopters', but these opportunities tend to be much greater in bureaucratic organisations with line management structures, in which promotion is largely on the basis of administrative responsibility; and much more restricted in the old traditional universities where promotion is on the basis of excellence in research and scholarship.

Overlaying these traditional – and still prevalent – organisational types in higher education, the political debate over the last decade has moved higher education institutions more towards being kinds of enterprises. Both ideologically and in practical terms, there are many forces impelling universities towards an enterprise culture. Some are recruiting students from all over the world, and staff may be spending their time crossing the globe to teach parttime masters degree courses in different countries. Some are recruiting many more mature students, often parttime, and are working closely with local business and industry. These changes in our system of higher education are important and exciting, but they imply a change in the culture. In particular, they do not fit easily with the pseudodemocracy of patronage and restricted collegiality.

There is a need for more rapid procedures for decisionmaking and for systems that can support the quick action stream of the entrepreneur. Almost all higher education institutions are changing their culture in line with the shifts in political ideology over the last twenty years. In trying to promote innovation it is important to be able to analyse this process of culture change in the organisations where we work. It helps to understand the fury that individuals often experience when they find themselves pushed by the imperatives of a different value system from the one that has underpinned their work over many years.

The critical component of organisational culture is its underpinning system of values, so that a change in culture equates with a change in values. In UK during 1996 a confidential report from the Higher Education Quality Council (HEQC), leaked to The Times Higher Education Supplement (THES), revealed a crisis among academics about the values of the system they were working within. According to the THES, the report said that research had found 'a considerable confusion over the nature and significance of UK first degrees'. Most academics consulted by HEQC 'seemed unclear whether a graduate today should be expected to possess the same general characteristics, specialist subject knowledge, or capacity for future development as fifteen years ago'. The report concluded that there was a need for institutions to be more explicit about what achievements are being judged, the distinctive character of particular degrees, and what is the minimum satisfactory level of performance or 'threshold' standard.

This crisis of confidence is an important part of the context for the ICT innovation in higher education. The uncertainty is by no means all bad. It provides an opportunity for redefining the nature of knowledge and breaking down the isolation of the traditional 'ivory tower' style university. Within the redefined university it is possible to give credit towards a degree not just for demonstrating conceptual 'academic' knowledge, but for experiential knowledge acquired in the workplace, for example for the generic competencies that are an essential characteristic of expertise in management. As a tool for teaching and learning, ICT has the potential to support the acquisition of these new kinds of knowledge. Within the redefined university .ICT has a part to play in redefining the nature of knowledge and radically changing the style of teaching.

An apparently innocuous change in technology may emerge as a serious threat to an organization because it would force it to transform its theory and structure. Technological, theoretical and social systems exist as aspects of one another; change in one provokes change in the others. And change in organizations has its impact on the person, because beliefs, values and the sense of self have their being in social systems. Schon's attack on bureaucracy and on the processes of 'dynamic conservatism' which make social systems 'self-reinforcing', reads like a rationale for the radical iconoclasm of British government policy in the 1980s.

Indeed it is certain that the ideas he presented in his Reith lectures on the BBC, and later published in Beyond the Stable State, raised considerable interest and led to wideranging debate. There is also general agreement in the research literature that innovation goes through stages. According to Fullan's classic study, there are four stages:

— First the approach, when the innovation becomes known to potential participants leading to a period of negotiation, during which they decide whether or not to become involved.

— Then a period of adoption, in which participants begin to use the new resources and make a preliminary assessment of the opportunities they offer.

— Next the implementation stage, when the innovation is put into practice; at this stage, the innovation inevitably goes through a process of adaptation which may or may not subvert its original purpose.

— Finally, if the innovation has not been rejected during any of the previous stages, comes the stage of continuation or institutionalisation, in which the innovation becomes fully integrated with the routines of practice and achieves permanency, insofar as that is ever possible.

Fullan's research shows that many innovations fail to reach the stage of institutionalisation, and many are only partially implemented or are largely subverted to better suit the values and practices of those required to implement them. There is a pattern of passive resistance and incremental withering of the initiative. Fullan's main concern is therefore to look at the features which support innovation and enable it to overcome these barriers. For each stage he identifies likely problems and suggests strategies for tackling them, drawn from research evidence. He stresses the importance of the roles of all the different players and identifies the following characteristic features of successful innovation: staff development and participation, good relationships between teachers, support from the head, a clear timeline, good communications and an internal consultant to support teachers.

As an alternative to this six stage model another one was proposed by Somekh et al. According to this model

— Orientation is the stage when participants seek out information about the innovation.

— Preparation comes next when participants are getting ready to begin.

— Routine is the first stage of implementation when participants establish lowlevel, routine use.

— Refinement is the stage when participants seek to refine and improve their use of the innovation.

— Integration is the stage when participants take steps to integrate their use of the innovation fully into their practice.

— Creative Integration is the stage when participants seek more effective ways of using the innovation, going beyond what has been achieved by others.

This is a useful model when analysing the experience of individuals, particularly in explaining why an innovation can 'get stuck' at the stage of lowlevel routine use; in terms of using ICT for teaching and learning in higher education, this is minimalist use without achieving any change in the nature of teaching and learning. To go beyond this stage, participants need to do a lot of creative work refining their use, thinking it through, changing it, integrating it much more seriously into what they were doing before. What makes this stage both fascinating and difficult is that integration should change both sides of the equation; i.e. what was done before should be changed to integrate with the innovation, just as much as the innovation should be changed to integrate with what was being done before.

It is only at the stage of integration that the innovation ceases to be an addon. At the final stage of creative integration – which only a few will achieve – the innovation is being used in ways that have not previously been envisaged. It is this creative potential that makes the process of innovation so appealing to some people. It is common for people to experience a sense of panic in trying out new things, but some people do get a buzz out of the adventure of innovation, and providing support for those embarking upon the use of ICT innovation is partly about trying to enable them to experience a buzz rather than panic.

When ICT is introduced, what does that actually mean in terms of what it is like to be a teacher? Most people who teach have some kind of love of the job – a sense of personal meaning in what they do. Some of that will relate to their discipline, to what it is they are teaching, and what counts as knowledge in that discipline. Some of it will be what they have found useful and successful to do over the years. They may actually enjoy the way that they enter the lecture room and the way that they stand at the overhead projector. Probably they experience an intellectual payoff from preparing a lecture, a buzz from feeling that this one is going to go really well tomorrow. Probably they get a buzz from their relationships with students, and depend to a considerable extent on watching students' faces, perhaps on seeing if they can get a laugh, to provide confirmation of their own value as a teacher.

The move to ICT is very disruptive to a lot of these things. So, in asking people to adopt the use of technology in their teaching, we may be asking them to abandon a lot of what, over the years, has made teaching rewarding for them. Moreover, institutions are very territorial places. Individuals often feel a sense of ownership of the rooms where they teach. Using ICT may require them to go into rooms which are part of a more alien culture. There may be some potential loss for them in terms of their formal or informal status in the organisation. Very importantly, the introduction of ICT requires a high level of collaboration: collaboration in course design, teaching in teams, joint development of resources and sharing of resources.

ICT is going to be used as an alternative to your input as a teacher, rather than perceiving yourself as having a creative role. ICT is not value neutral. Computers look as if they came out of the science or engineering laboratory, which they did, and for some people in disciplines like sociology, anthropology and English, that may be a not insignificant barrier. For them it may be very hard to feel good about using that kind of equipment in their teaching, and .working in a space whose alien feel may be reinforced by the title of 'laboratory'. The ICT innovation cuts across the established patterns of discourse that give members of each group a sense of meaning and identity, of belonging to a club. People instinctively feel anxious about working closely with people who use a different set of words.

The ICT innovation in higher education has the potential – some would say the obligation – to challenge existing pedagogical practice. If ICT is to be used effectively there are many decisions to be made.

— *Resources.* What should be the level of resources available for students? What would be costeffective now? Should every student be required to have a personal computer? Should every student have an Internet address? In some universities they already do, not in all. Should they all have unlimited access to the Internet? What would that cost? Who would pay for it? Can we really talk about effective use of ICT unless learners do have that kind of level of access?

— *Tasks.* What exactly are we doing with ICT? What is the nature of the learning task? Are we replacing lectures with some kind of interactive experience, or some creative experience, or some kind of information-seeking experience? If so, are those tasks really beneficial for learning, or is some of it time-consuming and not as efficient, perhaps, as the lecture, which in some senses is a very efficient way of 'one to many' teaching.

— *Teaching.* How does ICT change the nature of the teacher's role? In what ways can ICT bring new kinds of job satisfaction to teachers? How can we integrate interpersonal support for students with teaching methods that make use of ICT? What is the impact on teaching and learning if students have problems accessing the course website?

— *Course Organisation.* Should the organisation of teaching change to make better use of ICT? For example, should there be fewer lectures –more selfstudy – enlivened and extended lectures – tutorial support for selfstudy – occasional small group work?

— *Assessment.* Does ICT make it possible to change assessment practices radically, for example by an increase in machineread tests, more use of multiplechoice approaches, and more formative selftests in addition to summative assessment? How would changes of this kind be likely to affect the kind of knowledge that is tested?

Amongst a whole range of difficulties, two problems seemed particularly intractable because of the way in which they challenged institutional culture. The first related to course design.

Individual lecturers who were keen on using ICT in teaching were not going to be effective unless the whole structure of the course changed. Without a highlevel decision and agreement on collaborative action, it was inevitable that whatever ICT courseware was developed would be an optional extra that students could or could not use if they wanted to, in addition to the ongoing course. To introduce effective use of the kind of ICT resources becoming available necessitated radical change, of a kind that most of those trying to promote the ICT innovation were powerless to bring about. The second related to the fundamental purpose of assessment. Is the purpose of assessment to give feedback to students and thereby enrich their learning experience, or is assessment mainly for credentialing purposes, to sort students and categorise their level of success or failure?

Most of the work on the advantages of using ICT in assessment assumes the former, but the culture and traditions of universities are deeply rooted in the latter. There is considerable enthusiasm among academic staff for computer-assisted assessment, because of the increase in the assessment load that has resulted from the worsening staff-student ratio and semesterisation. But when it is assumed that the purpose of assessment is to categorise students' level of success and failure, the practical problems often appear insurmountable. Can you really have people sitting in a computer laboratory doing assessment on screen and ensure that they will not cheat? Can you really assess students while they have all those resources on their laptop, including access to the Internet? Again, they might cheat by just finding the references and reading them while they are doing the exam.

It is very difficult to see how there can be any radical change to the nature of learning while university – and national – culture makes these assumptions about assessment. However, it is at least helpful that the introduction of ICT is challenging this culture by introducing ways of making formative assessment a more integral part of learning. The outcomes will probably be a more balanced approach with some assessment for both purposes, but it is important for those introducing ICT to be aware of the distinction. So what can we say is successful use of ICT? To begin to grapple with this question we need to consider at least five different structural 'levels' of increasing complexity: students; individual lecturers; course teams and departments; the university as a whole; and alternative, 'virtual' higher education organisations. First there are the individual students. Is it sufficient for all students to have basic ICT tuition? A lot of universities now provide this and make some routine demands upon students to use ICT, for example to word process assignments.

If there is to be any major impact upon the learning opportunities of students, the next structural level, the course team or department, must be involved. This is the level at which it will be possible to plan changes to integrate ICT skills with module outcomes, and to begin to release resources to enable radical changes in teaching strategies. ICT can never be effective as an optional extra to existing pedagogical approaches; to be effective, ICT-related activities need to become an integral part of the planned delivery of modules by a department or team, requiring students to carry out ICT-related tasks as an obligatory part of their learning. This, in turn, has implications for the restructuring of universities.

## Computer Conferencing in Higher Education

Computer conferencing is part of a software family known as 'groupware'. It allows groups of people to participate in a shared discussion by posting messages which are stored on a central host computer for others to retrieve and comment upon. There are five key attributes that distinguish computer conferencing as a unique tool for education. They are:

— many-to-many communication;

— place independence;

— time independence;

— text-based;

— computer-mediated interaction.

Related to these collective characteristics, researchers and theorists suggest computer conferencing presents a new paradigm , a new domain of education and a new learning environment that is distinct from other forms of distance education and face-to-face learning.

As a mediating tool, computer conferencing facilitates two-way interaction among participants, thus enabling a classroom situation to be simulated on-line. The virtual classroom has many explicit and implicit characteristics that distinguish it from its face-to-face counterpart and present new challenges for educators.

According to researchers and theorists in the field, computer conferencing does not represent a mere shift in venues; rather it introduces a new set of social dynamics, problems and opportunities for teachers and learners. Dramatic claims are made about its potential to break down traditional barriers of education, connecting students to resource-rich, collaborative and democratic environments. While such assertions may be promising to educators and students, they also represent a tendency within the literature to confuse the medium's technical potential with it as an approach to teaching and learning.

A number of scholars hail computer conferencing as a medium that offers equal opportunity for participation and thus challenges the traditional power relationships between teachers and students, shifting control from the teacher to a more democratic group orientation. Claims of this nature are generally based upon studies of response levels and distribution of turn-taking in computer conferences. For example, Harasim studied computer-conferenced seminars at New Jersey Institute of Technology, and found that teachers contributed proportionally fewer responses than students and far less than classroom-based instructors. She states: 'In a face-to-face class, an instructor might monopolize 60-80% of verbal interaction, while a computer-mediated communication instructor might only contribute 10-15%'.A study by Graddol at the Open University in the United Kingdom (UK) supports Harasim's findings about the relative horizontal distribution of responses in their courses which use CoSy computer conferencing software.

The potential of computer conferencing to promote high and equal levels of student participation is advantageous to teachers who favour group collaboration and student-centered discussions. However, research on this issue is young and several studies contradict egalitarian claims. Some of the most frequently asserted advantages of CMC are the flattening of hierarchies, the consequential expansion of participation, and the channeling of attention away from the messenger and onto the message. The interviewees had some sympathy with this point, but generally seemed to have adopted systems for reconstructing status.

The removal of physical and verbal cues may reduce initial social bias, but, As the conference progresses, participants attach certain characteristics to messages, and this leads to differences in the status of participants.

Active cliques of students within computer conferences tended to monopolize conversation and inhibit other members from joining in. In the conference transcripts they analyzed, 50% of the comments were made by 10% of the participants.

The group interaction made possible through computer conferencing has generated interest in this medium as a tool for active learning, collaboration and constructivist teaching.

Computer-mediated communication is particularly suited to collaborative learning because 'the medium facilitates information exchange and provides the shared space essential for group work'. In fact, the literature on computer conferencing is heavily biased toward such learning models.

The self-pacing made possible through asynchronous communication and the act of articulating one's thoughts in writing promoted thorough and well-formed responses on-line. The new technologies have contributed to a movement away from a traditional objectivist paradigm that views education as the transmission of information from teacher to student, to one that views knowledge as a personally constructed world view. The collaborative potential of computer-mediated communication makes it an ideal tool for constructivist teaching. Distance educators can and should take advantage of this potential and encourage students to make their own meanings through collaboration with others.

Notable researchers on computer conferencing assert that the asynchronous group interaction of the medium demands a shift in the teacher's role from information presenter to facilitator of discussion Unlike traditional classroom activity, in which the teacher directs the instruction, leads the lessons, prompts responses, and paces the class, on-line group learning is student centered and requires a different role for the teacher, of facilitator rather than lecturer. The teacher plans the activities but then follows the flow of the conversation, offering guidance as needed rather than strictly adhering to the preplanned agenda or syllabus.

The rhetoric tends to simplify complex and varied teaching and learning models prevalent in classrooms today (physical and virtual) into two polarized camps: traditional, didactic, teacher-centered instruction that supposedly dominates face-to-face classrooms versus active, collaborative, student-centered learning environments possible through computer conferencing. While this rhetoric may help to dramatize the authors' points, it does little to help understand the complex pedagogical issues involved and factors related to or influenced by the medium. Teachers who favor student interaction and group discussion in their classrooms often have an easier time adapting to the on-line environment.

Rapid exchange of written communication creates a unique form of expression. The juxtaposition of personal exposure which results through on-line participation and the relative anonymity of faceless contact creates a 'new social space' that has its own set of dynamics. People are able to manage the presentation of their identity in more deliberate ways, taking time and editing messages to convey a certain tone. Thus, the on-line personality, Feenberg contends, is profoundly modified through self-conscious editing. Reflective thinking is a positive outcome of text-based interaction cited by researchers.

Written communication is a 'meta-cognitive skill' that gives occasion 'to make explicit to oneself the aspects of an activity that are usually tacit'. That is, the act of writing forces one to articulate, with enough clarity to be understood by others, personal thoughts and in so doing, helps the writer to examine their own reasoning process. Computer conference software stores all contributions in a database for participants to retrieve and review at their convenience. The transcript, as an evolving artifact of the online discussion, is a significant resource for learning. Students reported increased aattentiveness to written contributions over verbal exchanges in face-to-face classrooms and found the transcript offered complete notes that were impractical to track in a live discussion.

Text-based communication lends the opportunity for students to improve their writing skills. However, in a study of factors related to students' 'readiness' for computer conferencing, The medium 'presupposes the ability to read, write and type well'. Instead of presenting an opportunity for equal and unbiased participation, the narrow bandwidth of written communication may present a formidable barrier for weaker writers. Another potentially negative aspect related to text-only communication is the 'information overload' that results from the volume of text that accumulates as the discussion progresses. Students also perceive a loss of personal contact and clarity of message due to the lack of physical presence, voice intonation, gesture and other tacit cues

The traditional academic emphasis of evaluation on written work may cause participants to be overly selfconscious about the quality of their online messages and inhibit spontaneous expression.

The research on computer conferencing is relatively new to mainstream educational literature. The issues addressed in this narrow yet growing body are widespread and frequently illdefined. There is a tendency within the literature to confuse the potential of computer conferencing as a medium and a tool of education with it as an approach to teaching and learning. The problem of confounding medium and method becomes even more confusing when the discussion of computermediated communication is tied to a particular educational paradigm (namely collaborative learning models and contructivist teaching, as is commonly stressed throughout the literature).

Authors occasionally point to teaching strategies and student input as salient factors in determining the extent to which the potential of the medium to promote collaboration was actualized. However, most lose sight of these factors in their conclusion, favoring dramatic claims about the medium's inherent promise for progressive education.

Despite the medium's inherent support of a learnercentered environment, there is still a possibility that old patterns of teaching and learning will predominate. Tutors who were meant to be facilitators and resource people, available to be consulted when needed, might end up, with the complicity of their students, reproducing the social role of the classroom teacher as authority figure. This goes against the potential of [computermediated communication] for promoting the educational use of 'many-to-many' communication because it puts the teacher at center stage. Is it not possible that computer conferencing, like other classroom tools, is simply at the service of its users and therefore dependent upon the educational approaches employed? Similar questions surround claims about the egalitarian nature of the medium and the shifts in teaching roles that are proposed.

Many features of computer conferencing promoted in the literature – interactivity, collaboration, reflection, and self-direction are not inherent in the medium, instead this medium can be passive, didactic, competitive, spontaneous, and other-directed. Student participation, course design and instructional style are some of the salient factors that impact whether these elements emerge. The promise of computer conferencing for increased reflection, collaboration and intellectual amplification are largely dependent on the individuals who meet in these 'electronic classrooms'.

## ICT tools: Challenges in Classrooms

With the widespread use of information and communication technologies (ICT), there is understandable interest in the impact of ICT on teaching and learning. Although it is often claimed that computer technologies and the Internet have the potential to change both teaching and learning, teachers have been subjected to public pressures to use new technologies before they, and we, have a clear understanding of their impact on classroom practices and student learning.

Schools and classrooms are being equipped without adequate research or attention to the professional preparation of teachers. The belief that classrooms should be equipped with technology is predicated on the belief that technology can improve the rate, quality, amount, and effectiveness of learning. Although attractive, this belief must be tested with sound research. It is thus critical that the available research be assembled, reviewed, and critiqued as a prelude to pinpointing areas of future research and policy development.

Many studies show that preschoolers are "learning optimists" who rate their own abilities highly, underestimate task difficulty, and hold positive expectations of success. During middle childhood, children begin to distinguish ability, effort, and external factors in explaining their performance. How they attribute success and failure on tasks influences the likelihood of developing an intrinsic motivation to persist at challenging tasks and the development of effective metacognitive skills. This in turn influences performance on academic tasks.

*Attitudes*: Research supports conventional wisdom indicating that students who are positively disposed toward tasks or subject matter are likely to learn more and learn more easily. For this reason, student attitudes toward computer use could have an impact on their learning. Only one finding in the research on attitudes is clear: Children who are exposed to computers have a more positive attitude towards computers than those who are not.

Positive attitudes towards technologies allow for their productive use throughout life. Another finding is also relatively clear: Despite years of initiatives to engender positive attitudes among women toward ICTs and improve their efficacy in using them, men and boys still have a higher computer self-efficacy and more positive attitudes towards computers than girls and women. This discrepancy remains despite the reported use of computers in school rising to a non-gender differentiated level. It seems that simple exposure to computers does not guarantee positive attitudes towards them, or at least the positive attitudes are being mitigated in girls and women.

The gender discrepancy is being reduced, but much more slowly than predicted. Gender differences have several implications. On a very basic level, it has been argued that the software most commonly used does not appeal to girls as much as boys, and should therefore be structured differently. On a social level, differences in attitudes have ramifications for school performance and achievement, especially in the context of group work. This topic will be discussed more fully in the section devoted to achievement below.

*Attributions*: Positive attributions of academic success fuel a sense of mastery and are part of a positive cycle of learning that is associated with academic success. In this cycle, successes are attributed to ability and internalized while failures are discounted and attributed to situational factors beyond the control of the learner. In contrast, negative attributions of academic performance can give rise to learned helplessness, which is associated with poorer school performance. In this cycle, successes are discounted and attributed to luck while failures are internalized as indicators of low ability, leading to an overall sense of helplessness and failure. Students with learned helplessness perform less well on academic tasks than students who attribute their success to their own abilities.

Attributions to ability versus luck are also related to gender differences, making the area an important one for research. Despite the vast body of research on this topic in general, there is a paucity of work investigating how these cycles are manifested in relation to computer technologies. We could find only two studies on this topic. The first demonstrated that attributions to ability and task difficulty had a more significant effect on performance than attributions to luck and effort on computer tasks. The second study investigated the effect of gender on children's reactions to success and failure on computerized tasks. It found that boys were more likely to attribute failure on the tasks to unstable and external causes than were girls. In contrast, girls were more likely to attribute success on the tasks to unstable and external causes .

*Achievement orientation*: There have been a number of recent large analyses investigating whether access to a computer or use of a computer in instruction improves academic achievement. An analysis conducted by Statistics Canada using data from Ontario's Education Quality and Accountability Office's province-wide tests. These data were gathered in 1997 from 115 000 third graders in Ontario's English-speaking schools. While other factors such as smaller class sizes were found to be related to higher academic achievement, this study found no relationship between the presence of a computer in the classroom and the achievement of third grade students. In the United States, similar work has been done looking at the results of National Assessment of Education Progress (NAEP) tests. These tests, administered nationally every two years in mathematics and reading alternately, assess the effect of a number of variables, including computer use, on academic achievement.

The most recent analysis available used the scores on the reading test for students in grades four and eight. The analysis revealed that students who used computers in the classroom at least once each week do not perform better on the NAEP reading test than do those who use computers less than once a week. This was true even accounting for the comfort and training with computers that teachers reported: The analysis was restricted to teachers who reported that they were moderately well prepared to use computers for instructional purposes.

There are many examples of innovative programs combining access to technology with instruction designed to complement the new technological resources. Woodrow and colleagues have longitudinal evidence of the effectiveness of technology-enhanced instruction in a secondary science environment. In particular, they report on the experiences of high school students in a multimedia environment in Physics and Science classrooms. They have a substantial amount of data collected through interviews and questionnaires that indicate that the students enjoy working in the multimedia environment and believe that they are learning specific knowledge and general learning skills in a way that would not be supported by traditional instruction

Positive relations between computer use and achievement as a function of exposure to computer assisted instruction have been reported by Renaud, who looked at science performance of seventh grade low achievers. Similarly, van Daal et al. reported dramatic increases in reading and spelling performance of kindergarten students who were exposed to a computer-based reading and spelling program over those not exposed to a computerized program. In addition, one very well controlled study found a clear, positive relationship between the use of hypermedia instruction and achievement in engineering courses. There is thus some empirical support for a positive effect of technologies on student performance.

There has been a long-standing argument that the use of computers for instructional purposes increases motivation in children. Children without access to a computer at home will find it more motivating to go to classes where they have the opportunity to use a computer. Although intuitively reasonable, they offer no experimental support for this statement. Children using computers were highly motivated to complete their assignments and demonstrated high levels of curiosity, achievement orientation, and personal ownership of the project.

The use of technology in Israeli classrooms in high school increases pupils' self-efficacy and motivation to study and succeed. These motivational effects are also extendable to therapeutic settings. Similar results have been found with eighth and ninth grade science students. Unfortunately, none of these projects had a control group of students that did not use computers. One study that did have a control group showed no significant effects of computer work in task achievement of seventh and eighth graders, but the students did report valuing the computerized task more than the non-computerized control task. Other work refutes this argument, however.

Group work with the use of a computer does not by itself increase learning or satisfaction, but rather aspects of social facilitation and the collaboration process underlie many of these results. Third grade pupils working in groups on computer tasks have higher levels of interaction and, unlike other tasks, most of these interactions were concerned with solving the problem. When asked, children in her study reported that the limited time they had on the computer required them to focus on the task at hand, thus concentrating their efforts and encouraging on-task interactions.

There are few studies on how computer systems and learning environments are designed, constructed, and maintained. Stuve reports on a three year descriptive case study in which he explored the role of technology in the classroom after it had been installed, that is, how it was used by both the teachers and the children over several years. He found that specific features of the classroom environment, for example the location of the printer in relation to the class and the quality of the computers, had important impacts on how projects were structured and how learning activities were maintained. He argues that the realisation of technological innovation is socially constructed, with a complex interaction among students, teachers, and the physical and social environments supporting the technologies. This is the only study we could find that investigated this issue. Although it is a well-documented study, its descriptive nature does not permit hypothesis testing. It is imperative that more rigorous experimental research be done on this area. The design of the learning environment also includes the ratio of computers-to-students, affecting the size of learning groups that can be formed.

The nature of hardware and software affects both its use by and its impact on the learner. The design of hardware and software must take into account both motor and cognitive skill differences between children and adults. Low-level design details such as number of mouses and type of mouse had significant effects on children's performance and motivation.

There is as yet very little comprehensive or rigorous research investigating the software design and the effects of design features on student learning and performance. Although the role of visual presentation in information processing is well understood, increasingly sophisticated auditory presentations require further investigation. His preliminary findings suggest a role for both auditorally and visually complex programs and interactions. The use of multiple windows in complex tasks helps fourth grade students complete their work better than the use of single window presentations.

Gender plays a significant part in the effectiveness of the design interface for kindergarten children. They found that boys preferred the use of navigational buttons when searching for assistance whereas girls preferred to ask for help. In addition, girls preferred scenes that changed slowly, incorporated text into the game, and were colourful with an emphasis on reds and yellows. Boys preferred scenes that changed quickly and emphasised blues and greens.

The software programs used in schools receive very poor evaluations, despite a clear understanding that instructional materials are more effective if their development has been informed by research. Metacognitive knowledge includes knowledge about the self, the task, and strategies for learning. Memory and general problem solving skills also play a role in the effective use of metacognitive resources. The development and implementation of successful metacognitive skills can significantly influence learning and scholastic performance. Group work is seen as one of the major places where computer use can add to traditional instructional practices. The participation that is required when children are grouped around a computer, as opposed to working in isolation at individual computers, can have a positive effect on performance

Peer based interaction at the computer allows for exploration of the relationships between cognitive, metacognitive, and social processes. In particular, co-operative learning on computers is argued to facilitate peer interaction and have implications for motivation, self-esteem, and social behaviours. The extent of group effectiveness, at least in the 9-12 age group, is determined by several crucial factors, including the degree of autonomy developed by students, type of negotiation within a group, and the extent to which pupils appropriate the task.

The task assigned has been shown to dictate whether more or less autonomy is desirable. For ninth graders in a physics classroom, too much autonomy diminishes learning about the data themselves. High levels of autonomy on difficult synthesis tasks (reading) were detrimental to the performance of the fifth graders they studied; even though more structured help was available through the computer program, the children chose not to use it to the detriment of their learning.

Student choice as to whether or not to use available structure can, at this age, result in diminished performance. Younger students, such as the five and six year olds perform better when there are adults mediating the learning and providing structure. With older students, however, greater autonomy can be positive.

In terms of the benefits of computer use, who is doing the work seems to be just as important as what work is assigned. The importance of the pupil-teacher interaction is crucial in determining the composition of groups to include the diverse personality and work types that encourage the best group performance.

Training children in social skills is a better determinant of computer-based problem solving abilities than either gender or group composition. Memory strategies such as rehearsal become more effective over time and lead to better retention of information. One of the major technological attempts to encourage the use of rehearsal strategies in learning, and thus better retention of information, has been the use of computer-assisted instruction (CAI).

There is a general argument that using computers makes pupils better problem solvers and autonomous learners by encouraging the development of independent thinking skills beginning as young as preschool .

Elementary students require more and more cognitive control over their artistic creativity as they develop, and thus programs should be devised that allow them this control while at the same time encouraging their artistic expression. The largest volume of research on the impact of technology in the content areas has been conducted on mathematics instruction. Mathematics instruction also has the longest history of using technology for instructional purposes and boasts several impressive systems and programs for the instruction of mathematics and mathematical concepts.

Student attitudes toward computers and computer related technologies improve as a consequence of exposure to them. The use of ICTs for group work can be beneficial if teachers are able to take into account the complex interplay among the age of the students, the kind of task, and the amount of independence allowed. An aspect of the educational setting that should not be overlooked is the age of the students, as the effect of computers on different age groups can be radically different.

# 3

# Multicultural Curriculum Transformation

The underlying goal of multicultural education is to affect social change. The pathway toward this goal incorporates three strands of transformation: the transformation of self; the transformation of schools and schooling; and the transformation of society. Every child comes to school with an ethnic identity whether these identifications are conscious or unconscious. This identification must be recognized and respected by the teacher. It must be the basis for the learning activities in the classroom. The point here is to acknowledge differences rather than ignore them.

It is equally critical that the children recognize and appreciate their own ethnicity and learn to appreciate those of the other children in the class. This recognition of individual ethnic identities is the beginning point, it is a connector of both the teacher to the student and the students to each other. It is the basic building block in the learning process which requires knowing where the child is relative to him/herself and the content to be addressed. This ethnic identification is a continual point of focus throughout the education process and is the basis for developing the next level of identification which is a national identification.

The development of the global identification provides the students with the opportunity to see how as a nation we fit into the world society. It allows students to better understand that the actions of a nation must not only be viewed in terms of the implications for that nation but what are the effects on the whole world. Children who have developed both a strong ethnic and national identity should have the perspective to also develop a global identification which should in turn make them better citizens of the world community. At this point in time it is important to realize that the identifications discussed above are hierarchial. In other words the curriculum and the learning needs to proceed by first recognizing the ethnic identity, then the national and finally the global.

The development of the latter are dependent upon the development of the former. It is also important that the individual identities are not static but continually evolving and so it is important for the curriculum to emphasize all three types of identities as learning progresses. The metaphor of the melting pot is no longer functional. We have to switch to either the toss salad or the stew. It allows us to focus both on the differences in the ingredients while at the same time the beauty of the whole. a good salad does not have a bunch of components that look, taste or have the same texture. The success of the salad depends not only on its looks but also on a lot of other factors including the taste, the freshness of the ingredients, the smells, the textures and the mixture itself.

The goals of multicultural education are: to have every student achieve to his or her potential; to learn how to learn and to think critically; to encourage students to take an active role in their own education by bringing their stories and experiences into the learning scope. to address diverse learning styles; to appreciate the contributions of different groups who have contributed to our knowledge base; to develop positive attitudes about groups of people who are different from ourselves. to become good citizens of the school, the community, the country and the world community; to learn how to evaluate knowledge from different perspectives; to develop an ethnic, national and global identity; and to provide decision making skills and critical analysis skills so the students can make better choices in their everyday lives.

Multicultural education may increase the resentment encountered by students who feel that changes in school traditions, curriculum, and academic standards are not necessary to get along and respect students from ethnic minorities. Since many institutions resist change of any kind, passive resistance on the part of the administration may simulate acceptance of the tenants of Multicultural education. Of course, excepting the tenants of multicultural education should be avoided with enthusiasm and optimism. Multicultural education must have, as its crux, the below defining characteristics to achieve its purposes for students, teachers, parents, and administrators of the school system: (a) a learning environment that supports positive interracial contact; (b) a multicultural curriculum; (c) positive teacher expectations; (d) administrative support; and, (e) teacher training workshops. If one of the features is absent, frustration and heightened resentment may occur as backlash behaviors multiply.

The effects of a positive multicultural climate may manifest in a number of ways, such as: (a) diminished pockets of segregation among students; (b) less racial tension in the schools; (c) increased ethnic minority retention and classroom performance; and, (d) inclusion of a multicultural curriculum. The multicultural educational environment should not be a microcosm of our present society, with regard to issues of diversity and tolerance. Many factors determine a successful multicultural atmosphere, but the features as outlined above may be important indications of success. Administrative support for multicultural education is critical. How can a house stand if the foundation is fragile.

Multicultural education will be as successful as commitment to it by school administrators. Regardless of the level of commitment programs initiated under the guise of multiculturalism must receive reinforcement from administrators who are accountable for the success of established multicultural initiatives. A key factor in any proposed multicultural initiative is curriculum development. A multicultural curriculum should be considered for several reasons: (a) provides alternative points of view relative to information already taught in most educational systems; (b) provides ethnic minorities with a sense of being inclusive in history, science etc.; and, (c) decreases stereotypes, prejudice, bigotry, and racism.

Educational institutions have been dictated too long by attitudes, values, beliefs, and value systems of one race and class of people. At its most fundamental level, multicultural education represents an orientation to schooling and the teaching-learning process that is grounded in the democratic ideals of justice and equality.

Justice and equality have always been the focus of schools, but there is a substantial body of historical and contemporary evidence which demonstrates that the schooling experiences of most students of color, as well as many white students from economically poor and politically disempowered backgrounds, are inferior to those provided to white students from middle class, politically dominant backgrounds.

Due to this disparity, proponents of multicultural education call for a studied restructuring of many of the long-standing policies and conventions of public schooling. There are five critical dimensions of multicultural education: content integration, knowledge construction, prejudice reduction, equity pedagogy, and empowering school culture and social structure.

i) *Content integration*: The goal of content integration is to expand the curriculum by incorporating contributions of diverse cultures into traditional disciplines of study. Arguably, this dimension is easily realized through technology. For instance, teachers at all levels have used the World Wide Web to extend the available learning resources. Electronic mail and multimedia technologies promote communication and interactions between diverse groups with the purpose of helping students learn more about content they study in subject areas as social studies, science, psychology, and even foreign language. Many educators who acknowledge potential benefits of a merger between technology and multicultural education call for updating the physical infrastructures of schools. In schools where such updates (i.e., re-wiring) have occurred, teachers are making widespread use of the internet and other computer-based technology. The knowledge and skills students acquire in these schools typically are being reinforced by computer availability and internet access in their homes. This reality contrasts sharply with that of students from poor/ working class backgrounds who attend schools where the notion of re-wiring for internet access may seem superfluous in light of the absence of basic resources. Nor are these students likely to have internet access at home.

ii) *Knowledge construction*: Knowledge construction dimension promotes critical literacy by examining the manners in which scholars and scientists contribute to their respective fields of study. Knowledge construction builds upon content integration by making explicit the worldviews and perspectives that inform knowledge claims. Similarly, it expands the legitimate sources of knowledge by helping learners recognize that their own experiences both within and beyond school are viable foundations for acquiring knowledge and skills. Teacher educators are being called upon to use technology to promote and reinforce the knowledge construction process. Part of acquiring facility in knowledge construction is understanding phenomenon from the perspectives of others. To this end, teacher educators are making use of Internet technology to promote more critical engagement with subject matter.

iii) *Prejudice reduction*: Prejudice reduction is about eliminating all forms of bigotry. Also, it involves promoting healthy personal identity devoid of the tendency or need to denigrate those who differ from self. Multimedia presentations and distance learning technologies are being used to establish learning exchanges between students of diverse cultural backgrounds and thereby reduce prejudice and stereotyping. Likewise, technology is being used to promote positive self-concept and foster positive relationships between students from diverse backgrounds in geographically diverse areas. Such efforts have included videoconferences, computer conferences, interactions on the Web, and e-pals. Technologies used with middle grade students have included interactive compressed video and use of two-way televised communication systems via telephone lines. Teacher education students are using distance learning technology, multimedia, and e-mail to engage in cross-cultural and diverse regional interactions with other prospective teachers.

iv) *Equity pedagogy*: Equity pedagogy is about equalizing opportunities to learn. It involves incorporating various strategies and techniques that attend to learning styles and intelligence types. Writers interested in the nascent relationship between technology and multicultural education are discussing the urgency of using technology to address the various ways in which learners from diverse backgrounds best acquire school knowledge and skills. Nevertheless, it is difficult to discern whether current efforts to merge technology and multicultural education are addressing this fourth dimension directly. Indeed, some writers are concerned that technology may inadvertently privilege certain ways of processing information while it devalues others. An important issue for many contemporary educators, particularly in the university setting, is whether internet technology is in any way superior to face-to-face instruction. It would appear that one advantage internet technology holds over face-to-face classroom format is in its ability to provide educators and students wide access to a cross-cultural professional and learning community. This can be accommodated through e-mail, bulletin boards, and chatroom sites.

v) Empowering school culture and social structure: Multicultural education proponents contend that in order to provide high quality experiences for all students, many traditional aspects of schools will need to be reconfigured. This is referred to as empowering school culture and social structures. Its ultimate purpose is to change the taken-for-granted policies and practices of schools that, while useful to some students, have greatly diminished the schooling experience for many others.

## Role of Internet Technologies

With online technologies, discourse communities are expanded to encompass interactions and collaborative exchange projects among peers from diversified cultural backgrounds. The expanded communities open opportunities for learners to interact with multiple perspectives that challenge their existing knowledge constructions and impose cognitive conflicts requiring negotiation.

With the new online tools and their potential to enrich learning experiences beyond the capabilities of a traditional setting come new challenges for educators and educational researchers. There seems to be a link between the technologies and authentic learning and collaborative learning in general; between technologies and student-centred, constructivist practices; and discussions in the literature examine those capabilities. However, educators are aware of the void in the literature of empirical reports testing the related hypotheses. Thus, there is an urgency to develop and implement research designs that accommodate the nuances of learning atypical of nontechnology, teacher-directed environments.

as well as to explore alternative instructional paradigms that optimise the potential benefits of online technologies for learning.

The internet is the world most powerful computer network connecting personal computers, sophisticated mainframes, and high speed supercomputers around the globe. Because a myriad of computers and programmes are part of the internet, incompatibility problems can result because information is created using different computers and software.

In 1989, a group of scientists at the European Laboratory for Particle Physics (CERN) in Geneva, Switzerland began developing an internet tool that would link information produced by all of the CERN researchers. The tool provided a way to link textual information on different computers and created by different scientists. The object was to overcome issues of incompatibility and utilise a new way of linking made possible by computers, called "hypertext". Rather than presenting information in a linear or hierarchical fashion, hypertext permits information to be linked in a web-like structure. Nodes of information can be linked to other nodes of information in multiple ways. As a result, users can dynamically criss-cross the information web using pieces in the order most convenient to them.

The CERN project resulted in an innovative front-end to the internet, now referred to as the World-Wide Web (WWW). The web provides users with a uniform and convenient means of accessing the vast resources of the internet. In 1993, the National Centre for Supercomputing Applications (NCSA), at the University of Illinois pushed the CERN scientists' idea further by creating a software tool called Mosaic. Mosaic is an easy to use graphical user interface that permits text, graphics, sound and video to be hyperlinked. Mosaic was the first of the internet tools that are now referred to as "web browsers". Other well-known browsers include Netscape and Microsoft's internet explorer.

Web browsers permit users to connect to the internet and facilitate accessing information located on another remote computer. The web browser links to the remote computer just long enough so that the information you need can be sent to your computer for you to view. Documents created to be viewed by a browser are formatted using Hypertext Markup Language (HTML). HTML solves incompatibility problems by using standardised tags which indicate such things as whether a piece of text should be plain, bold, italic, or linked to another piece of text. Pages of information on a computer formatted with HTML and accessible to someone with a web browser, are referred to as 'home pages' or 'web pages'.

The web have made the internet a more user-friendly environment. The ability to integrate graphics, text, and sound into a single tool means that novice users do not have to struggle with such a steep learning curve. In addition, organisations and individuals can create home pages independently and link to other home pages on their own computers or to pages created by others on different computer systems. The web can be used by the distance educator to build a classroom home page. The home page can cover information about the class including the syllabus, exercises, literature references, and instructor's biography. The instructor can also provide links to information on the web that would be useful to students in the class. Other links can access library catalogues or each student's individual home page. In addition, the home page can link students to a discussion list or listserv that set up for student communication. It is also a relatively simple matter to use the homepage to create forms that students can fill out and that will end up being sent to you as an e-mail message.

The web allows more opportunites of interaction. The interaction itself is categorised within a learning context with the purpose of task/instructional completion or social relationship building, with a mixture of both types of interaction being common. Interactions should involve complex activity by learners to include engaging and reflecting, annotating, questioning, answering, pacing, elaborating, discussing, inquiring, problem-solving, linking, constructing, analysing, evaluating, and synthesising. The levels of interactivity include: (i) interaction between participants and learning materials, (ii) interaction between participants and instructors/experts, (iii) interaction among participants, and (iv) management/feedback communications, Although content and social interaction are interwoven into highly interactive web-based courses, each will be discussed independently to further explain the role of both forms of interaction in a web-based course.

Content interaction is based on the theory of learning that is most appropriate to achieve educational outcomes within the course itself. In many web-based courses, multiple layers of learning outcomes exist, thus suggesting that multiple strategies may be incorporated into the course. Some courses may include an intensive case study, while maintaining a weekly schedule of online lectures and discussion sessions. Other courses may adhere more loosely to a semester-long simulation with its outcome being an explanation of findings and events. It is difficult to prescribe one best fit for content interaction, given the wide range of possibilities available on the World Wide Web.

It is important, however, to ground the design of the learning environment in solid theory and pedagogy, as distance learning has been criticised for having very little, if any, theoretical context. Hannafin, Land, and Oliver discuss grounded design as a context for dealing with the range of design decisions that best facilitate learning outcomes. Grounded design is defined as the systematic implementation of processes and procedures that are rooted in established theory and research in human learning. Social interaction is a key element in online learning. Given that the nature of online learning is anytime anywhere, the potential for isolation and frustration exist. The social interaction of the course must, at least initially, be designed into the course.

Through collaboration and communication, the opportunity for learning more about peers and connecting with them in non-task specific conversation is more likely to occur. Although social interaction may have very little to do with a course, it is still valued as the primary vehicle for student communications in a web-based learning environment. Non-task/content specific social interaction may include conversation in a chat room, inquiries about used textbook purchases, or questions about using a new version of a piece of software. When collaborative teams of students work toward project completion, there is still the need for relationship building in the learning community. Relationship building is a necessary component of collaboration and communication and the perceptions of the efficacy of this type of social interaction can impact the learning outcomes of the course.

By the very nature of social interaction, learners are directly able to foster content interaction.The overuse or misuse of interaction strategies can lead to boredom, overload, and frustration. It lessens the likelihood that students will be able to surmise what is important, and once again, frustration may occur when students perceive interaction as online busywork. The more interactive the web-based course becomes, the more complex it is to use. For novice distance learners, complexity may very well lead to more frustration and isolation. Future web-based tools hopefully will promote collaboration and interaction online in a much easier-to-use format.

For now, designers of web-based courses should weigh the frequency and the quality of interactions required that best facilitate the learning outcomes to be achieved, where frequency does not always equal quality. The attributes of web-based instruction should be filtered through the philosophy and pedagogy that is presumed appropriate for the course, preferably adhering to the grounded design approach suggested by Hannafin. Oftentimes, lists of strategies and tactics are provided as design suggestions for web-based courses. When suggested out of context, it is difficult to surmise how the online experience may be structured.

For example, in a list that suggests threaded discussions be used, there is still little detail as to how they are to be used within the learning experience itself. In a more behaviourist notion, threaded discussion may be used to elicit responses to given questions. In a situated learning environment, threaded discussions may be used to discuss influences on the environment with a scientist in an attempt to determine why native plants are not surviving. Instructional content is the central component of a web-based course, as this is where new knowledge, skills, and abilities are presented. Whether students learn declarative knowledge or participate in a large-scale simulation, the way in which knowledge is shared sets the stage for all interactivity within the web-based course. When given a choice, instructors many times will select land design instructional methods and techniques that are consistent with their theoretical and philosophical views. Instruction is presented either through an instructor-centred approach or through a more student-centred approach. There are times when one style of instruction is better than the other.

When the outcomes of instruction are to analyse, synthesise, or evaluate, or when ill-defined authentic problems are the focus, a more student-centred approach would best facilitate the learning outcomes. An instructor-centred approach would work well for instruction that is procedural, declarative, or well-defined in role and definition. Much of what exists online as web-based courses appears to have a strong instructor-centred influence. In much of the instruction, information is presented, examples are provided, practice exists, and in many cases, feedback is available through mentors and instructors. Student-centred learning is appropriate for outcomes of instruction that are focused on analysis, synthesis, and evaluation.

Student-centred learning provides interactive, complementary activities that enable individuals to address unique learning interests and needs, study multiple levels of complexity, and deeper, understanding. Using open-ended strategies for learning, such as situated, learning, learners will actively construct meaning to determine how to proceed. This student-centred approach fosters a greater responsibility for learning and requires students to be more self-regulated in their approaches to learning. In some cases, scaffolding is provided that will facilitate self-regulation, thus providing strategies that students can use to create unique approaches to complex problems.

Collaborative online learning environments is an obvious strategy for promoting interactivity. Many of the same factors that exist for campus-based students in collaborative groups parallel collaboration on the web. Topics such as group size, group role definition, group assignment and shared grading all are issues as well on the web. A collaborative group's members should be committed to the "group goal" and to maximising each other's learning. Johnson and Johnson suggest very strongly that groups do not become collaborative just because someone assigns them together as a group. An effective collaborative group requires positive interdependence, group and individual accountability, promotive interaction, and interpersonal skill.

Quality can be obtained through highly interactive courses. Occasionally, however, a strong collaboration component in the course may hinder some students' participation. If, for whatever reason, some students are unable to participate in collaborative, group building exercises, those students may be left to communicate with only the instructor or mentor. Many students complain about getting too much information online, not being able to follow concurrent threads in a threaded discussion, and not being about to keep up with multiple conversations occurring in chat sessions. Despite some of the negative student comments, much can be said about conversation and e-discussion. Written communication seems to be more reflective, as students have more time to compose their thoughts and articulate in the manner intended online.

Monitoring is essential for survival in a web-based environ-ment, even more so than in a traditional environment. This element of web-based design is not included, yet it is essential that work independently and can self regulate their own learning. Many cognitive strategies can be embedded within a web-based course, along with tips and ideas for time management and independent learning. Performance support can be defined as an electronic system that provides integrated access to information, advice, learning experiences, and tools to help someone perform a task with the minimum of support by other people.

Supporting performance for the technical and even motivational components of the course is important and must be considered when a web-based course is designed and presented. In addition to supporting entire programmes at a distance, performance support can also provide in course assistance. Peer-to-peer interactive communication is another type of multi-way interaction between individual learners and the faculty member and commonly between learners and the learning group. This features is most often implemented with text chat; more sophisticated communication options are implemented with voice communications. May allow selective interaction between learners and/or instructor, but control of the conversation is shared equally among all participants.

Web based delivery is attempting to address all three Learning Formats, with varying degrees of maturity and success. Successful distance education programmes seek to combine all three forms of learning in programmes of study. Development of web-based courses can be very demanding, and often quite different from developing other kinds of media. Most self pace web based training includes the following features:

i) *Copiers*: Outline and overview to tell learners what the learning is about, what the learning goals are, how long it will take and what instructors expect of them.

ii) *Body content*: Must read area where you put your introduction and explanations, procedures and instructions. But remember, most users don't like to read a lot of copy on the screen so keep it short, simple and to the point

iii) *Demonstration or practice*: Demo, practice the lesson or simulate an environment, where possible.

iii) *A self checking quiz*: It gives trainees immediate answers and scores is part of the value added of WBT.

iv) *Help desk*. Provide an e-mail address or phone number on your WBT pages so learners know where to get help.

Online learning provides access to a potentially vast new student population. For students, the attractions are convenience and flexibility. Students can schedule schooling around their everyday lives without being constrained by the rigidity of regular class hours and the necessity of being in a physical classroom. Faculty members, on the other hand, are apt to feel concern and anxiety about engaging in this most-talked-about but never-experienced online teaching. Integrating unfamiliar technology into one's instructional strategies can be stressful at first. Even good instructors who have experience using the internet for social and/or professional reasons can suffer from unexpected barriers to successful implementation, such as technology problems, student dropout, work overload, and overwhelming amounts of administrative housekeeping.

One of the top requirements for the success of distance education is the availability of quality faculty support. Post-secondary institutions commonly employ faculty development specialists to assist faculty members in their online course development. The number of these positions is growing at a fast pace. Developing an online course is a complicated and time-consuming process, with many new and unique elements for instructors. Without the help of support services, developing and implementing successful online course can be an uphill battle. The demands that developing and teaching online courses pose to instructors are unique and novel. The faculty development specialists must accommodate the increased support needs of faculty. Instructors are likely to approach the project with a fair amount of anxiety, which is justifiable.

In order to make the development process efficient and faculty-friendly, faculty development specialists must keep in mind the aspects of the course development process that facilitate success. The goal of many online courses is the creation of a learning community, one where students and the instructor collaboratively share responsibility for the creation of joint knowledge as they jointly share responsibility in addressing learning tasks. Students who thrive in this environment tend to be more introverted in face-to-face situations, those who reflect deeply, are self-directed in their learning and are intrinsically motivated. Learners need to see the value of such learning properties engendered by this environment as collaboration, constructivism, interactivity, reflection, self-direction, individualisation, and experiential learning.

In the web-based course, a number of new communication elements confront the learner and must be addressed: asynchronicity, multiple conversations, interactivity, information overload, and pacing. Other online characteristics, such as social norms, instructor relationship, student role, and the academic atmosphere, are largely carried over from other school experiences. Students take these factors into consideration in developing learning approaches to work effectively online. Some are directly related to the technology, such as means of processing online information, deciding when and how to contribute, expressing oneself through written communication, dealing with multiple conversations and a deluge of messages, and determining interactivity. Other learning strategies come from prior study patterns in school and work settings: setting goals, individualising assignments, managing time, establishing attitudes, and seeking and using feedback.

Beyond just providing technical support, virtual institutions are using their help desks to route urgent administrative or academic requests to the appropriate office for timely attention. Redesigning a course for web-based delivery can be quite involved, requiring a steep learning curve, especially where there is limited institutional support for this activity. When a regular teacher decides to accommodate some distance students as well as the classroom ones, she or he finds there is twice as much work if taught like two different sections of the course. Course developers and instructors are often part-time, adjunct faculty and may be doing this in addition to their other full-time jobs. To attend to all of the web conference areas can be demanding, especially when there are 15 to 25 students enrolled in a course. Some educators claim that the time involved in delivering an online course can be up to three times as much as a face-to-face one, but this need not be the case it teachers and students budget their online time. Due to the emphasis placed on student participation, teachers need to shift roles to facilitating and managing peer-learning, instead of lecturing or inserting themselves as often into the discussion as they might in the classroom.

There are institutions who have adopted an independent study model of web-based education that demands more investment in up-front course development, but can accommodate greater numbers of students without continual faculty involvement during delivery. For example, Brigham Young University's Independent Study programme allows students to start their courses on any date with a year to complete; they also provide automatic grading of web-based, multiple-choice assignments with immediate feedback. These courses are supplemented by related websites, multimedia resources on CD-ROM, and have optional online discussions with peers. The institutional dimensions of academic student support are similar to those faced by lower-tech delivery systems, but the college or university offering web-based courses needs to mount these services online.

The provision of a web-based programme was a chief reason distance students chose the institution, and it is the means by which students interact in their courses. They expect that other communications with the campus about academic and administrative matters will be online as well. These fuller academic supports go beyond single-course interaction, and therefore require programmatic responses like: online counselling for educational adjustments and advising for degree planning; assessment for prior learning; student discussion areas; online career centres; and access to academic resources via the internet to support their degree programme study. Students who lacked these environmental supports attributed their failure to external factors such as insufficient time, distractions, and circumstances that arose over which they had little control.

Readiness is the major component of successful online learning. Readiness includes personal factors such as a compatible learning style, proficient computer skills, an interest in the content of the course, mastery of prerequisites, and good reading, writing, and keyboard skills. It also include, such environmental factors as having a quiet, roomy study area, a social network of family friends, and work associates that value the student's educational pursuits, a lifestyle with existence within it for distance study, and technical/institutional assistance in place for obstacles that might arise. Institutions are obliged to present realistic and accurate information about course demands, but their marketing efforts sometimes overshadow this voice.

Effective counselling as the primary means of accomplishing this. This role, assumed by full-time counsellors, tutors and support staff means being supportive, encouraging, and pastoral to some extent. Such counselling sets forth realistic expectations about online study demands for working adult students who have been away from college and/or never juggled their education with other roles they must play. The counsellor suggests, needs to let students know that it is those who take direct responsibility and control of their college experience that prove to be most successful. This counselling can also address the readiness factors listed above and assist students with time management, organising their situation for a successful educational role and activities, and garnishing support from spouse, children, and their employer.

For many years distance programmes have accepted most standard forms of prior learning credit as it related to the student's degree programme, such as accredited college transcripts, CLEP test scores, and ACE, PONSI, and DANTES recommended credit equivalents. However, individualised credit by evaluation (CBE) was restricted to in-person settings. No longer will this be the case, however. SUNY-ESC's Centre for Distance Learning has begun individualised CBE in common areas, done at a distance through e-mail, the phone, and mail and such an web-based environment is being designed. Other virtual supports are social in nature, such as announcement areas, student bulletin boards, and topical conversation areas; these integrate students with their peers, create an online Community of scholars, and create institutional affiliation. The British Open University (BOU) Students' Association maintains several hundred such conferences covering the gamut of topics to bring together its student body. It operates a bulletin board for events and activities of student interest. A majority of adult distance students pursue further education for career advancement or change. These individuals are returning to college as necessity learners—where education is essential for them to keep or obtain a job—or as rainy day planners—where education provides a safety net to give them options if opportunities come up or something goes awry in their current position. Therefore, an important student service on the virtual college site would be a career centre. Such a centre could have such features as information about jobs and employment; career testing and counselling; networking about jobs with other students, university personnel, and alumni; as well as links to online job search services.

### *Web-based Interactive Educcation*

The web has the potential to transcend the capabilities of many other multicultural media in its supplemental value to multicultural teaching practices. The key for unlocking this potential lies in understanding and using the web not merely as an enormous compendium of informational resources, but more importantly as an interactive medium that can connect people across borders and boundaries.

With this in mind, there are clear intersections between some of the important ideals in multicultural curriculum transformation and the educational opportunities presented by the Web. A vast network of teachers and students around the world and across myriad cultures who have read a particular textbook, gathering somewhere to share questions and exchange resources on a given topic. The interactive opportunities can transcend the potential of most other educational media as a means to connect students with first person sources beyond classroom walls and national borders and across cultures.

Most Web site creators provide an email address and/or other contact information so that teachers, students, and others can, in fact, contact them with questions, challenges, critiques, or comments. Many educators understand Inclusive teaching as incorporating diverse voices and perspectives in the classroom. To them, inclusion is about finding materials and tools that are representative of the students in the classroom.

Multicultural education takes this concept a step further. If education is truly to be student-centered, then the experiences, perspectives, and ideas of the students themselves must be brought to the fore in the educational experience. To be "included" in the educational process, students, as well as teachers, must be given opportunities to have their voices heard and to hear each others' voices.

The Web is helping to facilitate this kind of inclusivity through countless sites that encourage teachers and students to participate in virtual global communities with other teachers and students who may be either very culturally similar or different. Collaborative and interdisciplinary teaching and learning are concepts that have been introduced, attempted, and reintroduced for decades. It is not uncommon for a group of teachers from a particular school to combine efforts in an attempt to connect lessons from subject to subject.

In fact, for many teachers who struggle with time constraints and burn-out, sharing resources and collaborative planning become vital aspects of day-to-day classroom operations. For others, it is an avenue for modeling constructive and cooperative bridge-building across groups. As with Interactive and Inclusive teaching and learning, the Web has the potential to greatly expand the breadth and depth of collaborative possibilities of educators. Despite the wonderful multicultural and educational potential the Internet holds, the very feature of the Internet that can facilitate Interactive, Collaborative, and Inclusive teaching and learning - interactivity - remains sadly untapped by educators.

Like no previous medium, the Internet can facilitate cross-cultural communication, interpersonal bridge-building, and intercultural networking. It can expand your resource base virtually infinitely and diversify it to a previously unthinkable extent. Below are some strategies for using the Internet to do just that - expand your resource base by networking across cultures, national boundaries, and even comfort zones. Several email discussion forums exist that deal specifically with multicultural education and related issues. Participants can post messages to a list address, and those messages are then circulated to the rest of the forum's subscribers via email. Like discussion boards, email forums provide participants with the opportunity to network with other people interested in a particular topic and to engage in challenging and thought-provoking dialogue on a variety of issues. Email forums tend to be more intimate and personal than discussion boards. Because people generally participate in email forums over a considerable length of time, the names and email addresses flashing into everyone's mailbox can become familiar. This can provide an opportunity to make more personal connections with other educators or activists from around the world.

The primary reason teachers give for not incorporating computer technology into classroom practice is a lack of training or knowledge about how to use products such as CD-ROMs and Web sites. Educators, already pressured by time constraints, are often intimidated by a perceived learning curve when it comes to developing better computer skills. For many, this feeling is exacerbated when they finally learn enough about the Web to navigate around cyberspace and do simple searches, and suddenly find themselves lost in a maze of broken links, pornographic sites, and educational sites that have little or no original content or that have not been updated since 1996. Several media and educational organizations are familiar for producing TV shows, films, CD-ROMs, books, and other teaching and learning materials that support multicultural ideals and curriculum development.

The National Geographic Society, the Discovery Channel, the Public Broadcasting Company (PBS) and others have been part of many of our classrooms for years. Like other educational organizations and companies, National Geographic, PBS, and others recognize that in order to remain competitive in today's market, they need to include a strong and visible Web presence among their multiple projects. As a result, they have developed a series of techniques and strategies for attracting Web users to their sites. One strategy many organizations employ to bring users to their sites is to provide free educational materials and resources. In fact, there seems to be a competition brewing among those companies known for producing educational media to offer more, and better, resources than their competitors. Teachers and students are among the winners of this competition, reaping the benefits of several sites scrambling to outdo their competitors.

There are hundreds of multicultural education links pages or general multicultural education pages that are comprised entirely of links to other sites. What makes these sites confusing and frustrating is that they are often linked to each other. A user can spend hours linking from one list of links to another, and so on, without ever finding original resources, teaching tools, or interactive opportunities. Most of the criteria used to assess and evaluate traditional educational media such as textbooks and films can be directly applied to Web sites as well. These include: accuracy of the information, critical analysis of possible bias, credibility of the author and/or publishing source, appropriateness and accessibility to the specified audience, timeliness, relevance to a particular subject area, validity of content, and effectiveness of aesthetic aspects.

Still, for a variety reasons, even deeper considerations for some of the more traditional educational evaluation criteria and several new criteria must be added to old models to holistically evaluate products of this fairly new cyber-medium. For instance, unlike traditional educational media such as films, textbooks, and journals that usually go through a rigorous review process before being made widely available to teachers and students, virtually anybody with access to a Web server can create an educational Web site. In most cases, there is no entity comparable to a publishing company to help ensure the credibility or expertise of educational Web designers.

Likewise, as is the case with many journals, there is no formal review board to examine the validity of the information on most educational Web sites. For the most part, the responsibility is left with the user to assess these issues. Other complications to the assessment of Web sites exist within the structure of the medium itself. In no other medium is the line between commercial and informational distinctions quite so blurry. Sometimes it is difficult to ascertain whether a particular site is a purely commercial venture or a purely educational venture. In fact, it might well be the case that no site fits the latter extreme.

Snce many Web sites are produced by unfamiliar sources, we, the users, must look deeper to uncover the bias of an educational Web site. In addition, unlike in books or films, the information on Web sites is not static. This can be a strength, allowing site maintainers and authors to continually update material. Literally hundreds of models for evaluating Web sites have been created by university librarians, educational and instructional technologists, and Web developers. Some of these focus on content credibility and validity while others focus on design and navigability. There is sometimes a tendency in education to use new technology for the sake of using new technology and without a particular need or sense for how it will improve curricula or pedagogy. As somewhat of a cautionary measure, this category may appear to be an obvious first step in assessing a Web site or any educational product. It explores the extent to which the content and target audience of a site match with your needs and target audience. One cannot assume credibility or expertise in regards to a Web site as readily as they might with a textbook. We must be conscious of credibility both in terms of the author's authority and the trustworthiness of a site's content. Again, this is a step that should be taken in relation to all educational media. It is not always so much about what information is included - we must remember to also ask what is nit included.

These criteria critically examine the inclusiveness of a site or whether the author is up-front about its exclusiveness. The foundation of a multicultural curriculum is accuracy and completeness. This category addresses both of these intertwined concepts.The internet was originally designed to give people access to each other and information. If a resource is inaccessible because of coding problems or incompatibility with certain browsers or special-needs users, it fails to meet even the minimum requirements for an effective educational tool. And if a site author or sponsor is inaccessible through the site, she or he fails to take advantage of the fundamental nature and value of internet technology.

Web has the capability to house educational opportunities consistent with the principles of multicultural teaching and learning to a greater extent than any other medium. Amidst all of the hype about the Internet is the reality of its inevitability. Forged by the competitive struggles of the private sector, it will soon surpass today's expectations like a Ferrari overtaking the Model-T. Web-based education is just beginning, with something of far greater promise emerging in the middle distance.

Access is more than getting one's hands on a computer, or simply connecting to the Internet. Access must be convenient and affordable. It must offer a user the opportunity to find and download complex, content-rich resources. The technology that supports access must be where the learner is located and be available whenever he or she needs it. Access may take place in the school or college or adult literacy classroom, in the library or after school center, in the community center or workplace, or in the home. Those who work with the technology that supports access must have the skill and understanding to apply it well. If the user-whether teacher or learner, parent or administrator-does not know how to work with technology or where to go on the Internet to find material of value, that learner does not have real access to what the Internet offers. Access also implies that once a user has the connection and is able to use it, he or she can find content and applications that have meaning and value for his or her learning needs.

Without broad access, there will be little demand for the innovative content and applications that can bring new teaching techniques and new assessment models. Without access, teachers cannot benefit from the just-in-time training and support the Internet has made possible in other professions. Without access, schools and universities will not have the links that could move research into practice and practice into research. In its purest sense, broadband refers to the transmission of large amounts of data electronically, whether through wire or wirelessly. The more powerful the capability to transmit data, the richer the online experience. For education, broadband access means the elimination of time and distance from the learning equation. Broadband carries with it powerful multimedia learning opportunities, the full interactivity of instructional content, and the quality and speed of communications.

Broadband access today is 50 to several hundred times more powerful than its precursors. Broadband access tomorrow holds even greater promise. The promise of widely available, high quality web-based education is made possible by technological and communications trends that could lead to important educational applications over the next two to three years.

The first trend is toward greater broadband access and better data packet handling capabilities resulting from the new "Internet2" project. For learners this will mean a richer delivery of content than today's delivery of simple text. Tomorrow, higher "bandwidth" will enable richer interactive environments.

The second trend is that of pervasive computing, in which computting connectivity, and communications technologies connect small, multipurpose devices, linking them by wireless technologies. It is much cheaper to build cellular relay stations than lay miles of cable. Wireless solutions may enable underdeveloped and remote areas to quickly take advantage of the Web via wireless phones, two-way pagers, and hand-held devices. Applications such as e-mail and the World Wide Web, initially developed to enable collaboration among researchers, have transformed the way we work and learn.Today, academia, government, and industry are once again working together to sustain the same partnership that nurtured the Internet in its infancy. This partnership is developing, testing, and deploying the high-performance Internet technologies required to enable a new generation of network applications."Internet2" and the Next Generation Internet (NGI) initiatives are among the efforts in this area. Internet2 is a consortium led by over 180 U.S. universities working with over 70 leading companies to develop and deploy advanced network applications and technologies for research and higher education. Internet2 members work closely with agencies participating in the NGI.

The third trend is digital convergence: merging the capabilities of telephone, radio, television, and other interactive devices. The ubiquitous infrastructure of television will be significantly enhanced by conversion to digital transmission. Through this increased capability, stations can offer dramatically enhanced programming by "datacasting" a wealth of supplemental information to accompany the regular broadcast. This may include course materials, software, and reference guides delivered via text, video, or audio formats. Direct satellite connections to the home offer another pathway for rich content.

The fourth trend accelerating the pace of educational technology advances is the establishment of technical standards for content development and sharing. Groups involved in developing learning standards are working together under the umbrella of the federal Advanced Distributed Learning (ADL) initiative. Led by the U.S. Department of Defense, with the cooperation of other federal agencies, academia, the private sector, and the technology industry, this group has developed standards for interoperability known as the Sharable Courseware Object Reference Model (SCORM). These standards provide a foundation for the Pentagon to build the learning environment of the future. The influence of this initiative will reach far beyond the military, as have past initiatives including the development of the Internet.

The fifth trend is the emergence of "adaptive technology"-technology that combines speech recognition, gesture recognition, text-to-speech conversion, language translation, and sensory immersion to change the very substance of network-enhanced human communication.

A final trend is the dramatic drop in the unit cost of broadband. Bandwidth will decrease in cost and increase in power more rapidly than the advances in chip technology. Ubiquitous Internet access can become a viable option for all, rather than a privileged few.

To benefit fully from these trends, learners must have affordable, easy access to the computing power necessary to bring these resources to the desktop, the laptop, or the appropriate Internet-enabled handheld-or even wearable device. To study responses to these trends in detail, let us look at the case of US, where internet is used for education more than any other countries in the woirld, In US, in just a year and a half the share of households with Internet access doubled. Broadband penetration is still greater in central cities and urban areas than in rural areas. Home access is important for students doing research, taking online courses, and communicating with teachers and other learners. For parents, online access means new kinds of communication with their children's schools, with their children's teachers, and with other parents. For all households, Internet access is another way to connect with their communities and government services. Home access helps to advance economic opportunities: low-income users were the most likely to report using the Internet to look for jobs.

Those learners without Internet access at home rely on schools, libraries, and other public places to provide this access. For households with incomes below $40,000, students are more likely to have Internet access at school. For many economically disadvantaged and minority group youngsters, a computer at school or in the library after school is the only link to the wide world of the Internet. Educational institutions are struggling to provide students with Internet access, and great strides have been made in bringing schools, libraries, and postsecondary institutions online. But here again, there are gaps.

The E-rate has been a major factor in providing school and library access. Enacted as a part of the Universal Service Program of the Telecommunications Act of 1996, the E-rate program provides discounts to public and private schools, libraries, and consortia on the costs of telecommunications services, Internet access, and internal networking. However, E-rate discounts do not reach places where many others could benefit from the learning opportunities of the Internet-from daycare centers to senior centers, and from adult literacy programs and community centers to museums, and other venues for both formal and informal learning.

The recent growth in Internet connectivity has been dramatic. In US, school connectivity has grown from 65 percent in 1996 to 95 percent in 1999. But what counts most for instructional purposes is classroom connectivity, providing student access to Internet connections where they learn-in the classroom. Classroom connectivity has soared from 14 percent in 1996 to 63 percent in 1999. Classroom access is still greater for the wealthy. Wealthy school classroom access almost doubles that of poor schools. And per computer access is no better: schools with the highest percentage of students in poverty average 16 students per Internet-linked computer. For wealthy schools the ratio is 7 students per computer, while the national average is 9 to 1. Poor schools need a significant investment to reach the ratio of 4 students per classroom computer considered a minimum level of access for effective use.

Postsecondary education institutions are also rapidly expanding student access to the Internet. Yet, there are institutional disparities. For example, 58 percent of all postsecondary students own their own computer. This figure varies from a high of 79 percent of students at private universities, to 34 percent of those attending private two-year institutions, and 39.6 percent of those attending public two-year institutions. The lower figure for community colleges is particularly troubling because community colleges- with their tradition of low tuition, flexible programming, open door admissions, and customized services-enroll proportionately larger percentages of the postsecondary student population, and larger percentages of minority students.

Among Americans of all ages, nearly 60 percent of those with a disability have never used a personal computer, compared with 25 percent of those without a disability. Among those with a disability, people who have impaired vision and problems with manual dexterity have even lower rates of Internet access and are less likely to use a computer regularly than those with hearing and mobility problems. Current laws mandate that recipients of federal funds cannot discriminate on the basis of disability. These laws have been extended to ban discrimination by any state or local government under the Americans with Disabilities Act.

Educational institutions receiving federal funds must offer equitable access to technology for all students. With the advent of adaptive technology, equity of access for disabled students is possible. Speech synthesizers and screen access software allow the computer to speak whatever text appears on its monitor, facilitating use for blind users. Audio components and simulcasts can be accompanied by real-time captioning.

Currently, there are basic design and development guidelines that are widely available and accepted by industry and consumers, through the Web Accessibility

Initiative of the World Wide Web Consortium. As a support for Web site developers, the Center for Applied Special Technology (CAST) created Bobby, a Web-based tool that analyzes Web pages for their accessibility to people with disabilities. CAST offers Bobby as a free public service in order to expand opportunities for people with disabilities through the innovative uses of computer technology. Once a Web site receives a Bobby approved rating, it is authorized to display a "Bobby Approved" icon. CAST also maintains a database of Bobby-approved Web sites. Universal designs are those that eliminate "gratuitous barriers" while adding functional equivalents. These universal design principles ultimately benefit all learners. They support what neuroscience and other learning research have shown us about learning-there is not one "typical" learner, just as there is not one path to learning.

A recent survey by the US National Education Association (NEA) found that most teachers have some facility using computers. Ninety-four percent of NEA members, and 99 percent of those under 35, are able to surf the Web. However, familiarity does not equal proficiency. Most do not know how to apply these skills in classroom instruction. Common sense holds that technology training for teachers will no longer be an issue if we can wait long enough for a new generation of younger teachers, raised on technology, to enter the profession. However, this is one common sense belief that simply does not hold up to close examination. Another survey found that young teachers' self-assessment of their ability to teach with technology was no different than that of their older colleagues. While younger teachers may have basic technology skills—they realize that they, like their older colleagues, do not know how to apply these skills to teaching.

The ability to use technology for non-instructional purposes does not necessarily translate into either the will or the capability to use technology to support student learning. Although they are not technophobes, these new teachers lack a clear conception of effective classroom uses of technology in their subject area.

Professional development is the critical ingredient for effective use of technology in the classroom. Seventy percent of educators polled regarding technology in instruction put professional development at the top of their list of technology challenges. They said what is needed is both the initial training for those just beginning to use technology and continuing education to support the growth of innovators. Three consecutive years of surveys in higher education showed the same thing: institutions ranked their greatest technological challenge as "assisting faculty to integrate information technology into instruction."

Professional development is often called "training," but the term implies much more than just building basic technology skills. It means developing a vision built on the understanding that technology is a tool that can offer solutions to longstanding teaching and learning problems. It is more than knowing how to automate past practices. It is the growing understanding that comes with confidence to "think with technology" in order to approach old problems in new ways. Almost two-thirds of all teachers feel they are not at all prepared or only somewhat well prepared to use technology in their teaching. Change is necessary on two fronts: in the preparatory (pre-service) education of teacher candidates, and in the continuing (in-service) education of those already in the education profession. Both groups need assistance and support in using the best tools technology offers to meet teaching goals and challenges.

The training teachers do receive is usually too little, too basic, and too generic to help them develop real facility in teaching with technology. Ninety-six percent reported that the most common training they received was on basic computer skills. A survey of public school teachers in US found that while most received some technology-related professional development in the 1998-99 school year, the training was basic and brief, lasting only 1 to 5 hours for 39 percent of teachers, and just 6 to 10 hours for another 19 percent of those trained. Teachers need more than a quick course in basic computer operations. They need guidance in using the best tools in the best ways to support the best kinds of instruction. And they need something more.

When asked in a National Center for Education Statistics (NCES) survey in US to name the greatest barrier to their use of computers and the Internet in the classroom, most teachers cited lack of "release time" (time outside classroom) to "learn, practice, or plan ways to use computers or the Internet." This factor outweighed their concern about too few computers or lack of time in the schedule for students to use computers in class.

The success of the private sector in integrating technology into its operations suggests a better approach for American education. In the business world, training is tailored, focused, and just-in-time. In the education world, it is more often one-size-fits-all, generic, and just-in-case. The overwhelming majority of all corporate and government training occurs on paid time. In public schools, teachers report just over a third of their professional development occurs on paid time.

Professionals in other fields expect to be trained regularly. Motorola, long the standard for industry, provides every employee with at least 40 hours of training each year. Equally significant, professionals in other fields are provided with follow-up support needed for that training to take root-including immediate access to the hardware and software on which they are trained, Internet connections, and easy access to support personnel and follow- up skill building.Many teachers have been trained on systems not installed in their schools. Many do not receive follow-up support.

Only 67 percent of teachers in the NCES survey reported that follow-up or advanced training was available to them. Most business professionals have personal computers provided to them at work and some industries give employees computers they can use at home. But K-12 teachers rarely are provided these benefits. Although 62 percent of teachers have access to a desktop computer while at school, only 28 percent have the ability to borrow one for occasional use at home. Most teachers are not rewarded or reimbursed for the time they spend in training. Just as some teachers spend their own money for classroom supplies, some teachers pay for their own preparation. Many take classes on their own time and pay their own tuition or fees.

Technology training rarely translates directly into higher pay for teachers. In fact, a growing concern among schools is the lure of higher salaries offered in the private sector to teachers and administrators who do exhibit strong technical proficiencies or a desire to develop these. There are other ways K-12 teachers are treated differently than professionals in business and industry. Intellectual support, as well as technical support, is rare.

A recent study in US found that only 13 percent of the US's teachers work in what could be defined as a "high quality technology-supported environment. For most teachers, technical assistance is limited, if available at all. Another study measuring technology support for district technology coordinators in 27 states found that it took from 14 hours to more than 7 days to fix a technology problem in a school or classroom. The average response time was more than two days. While this would be unthinkable in most businesses, imagine what it means to a teacher who has developed a lesson around the Internet, only to discover that the whole class is disrupted for an unknown period of time. It is simply intolerable. Fewer than 20 percent of all schools have a full-time technology coordinator. In most cases, technology coordinators are charged with training teachers and helping them integrate technology in their classes. In reality, they spend most of their time on technical support. On a weekly basis, full-time technology coordinators spend only 3 to 4 minutes per teacher assisting with technology integration.

Most of a teacher's day is spent separated from colleagues, with little time or opportunity to share in the give-and-take of problem-solving common in most office or work environments. For elementary and secondary education teachers, planning periods are few and often occur in isolation. Group meetings are focused on issues that affect the institution as a whole or the department or grade level, but they don't offer the opportunity to express the concerns or share the wisdom of the individual teacher. Teachers rarely have the opportunity to work with others to share their questions, concerns, and successes. Most are isolated and, unlike other professionals, have little access to the resources they need to stay up to date in their fields. In contrast, teachers in other countries are provided far more paid time for planning: Japanese teachers spend about 40 percent of their paid time on professional development and collaboration compared with about 14 percent for their American counterparts.

The Internet is making it possible to connect teachers to each other, giving opportunities for mentoring, collaboration, and formal and informal online learning. Traditional one-size-fits-all professional development workshops are giving way to a new, more teacher-centered, self-directed model of teacher learning. Through the Internet, teachers have access to high quality online professional development opportunities beyond what the local school or district is able to offer.

Online courses and seminars, follow-up consultations and mentoring, and collaborations with experts and peers can take place without the expense and classroom disruption created by repeated absences for face-to-face meetings. In working in online environments, teachers obtain a collateral benefit: they learn important technological skills.

## Role of Virtual Libraries

The library is a key component, of quality education, and academic institutions have a responsibility to provide external students with resources, facilities and services equivalent to their internal peers. The virtual institution must provide an online bookstore for students to order course guides, textbooks, and major instructional resources for their online course. Other resources could include lab kits, calculators, CD-ROMs, computer software, audio and videocassettes, and so forth. Such facilities will allow students to purchase materials by courses as separate components, paying for their purchases online by credit card.

Distance libraries allow online students to search databases that may only have citations and abstracts, and then allow them to retrieve the documents from their own collections for modest photocopying and mailing fees. For book check-outs, these institutions have an online circulation desk that allows for longer periods to compensate for postal mail exchanges. Libraries employ user identification and password procedures to ensure that only genuine students of the institution can use online subscription services for which it pays fees. The WGU has established an electronic reserve, putting an electronic version of an article or a chapter of a book on a password-protected website for a limited period of time. Often, distance students can, purchase access to a local academic library in their community or region for a nominal fee and use interlibrary loan services at their local library for books.

High quality academic resources are being made available through the web, but sometimes it is difficult for distance students to judge the academic quality of these sites. Distance educators should integrate information gathering and evaluation skills into the distance curricula as it has on campus. Additionally, libraries must get students familiar with their services and raise their expectations to use what online information resources are currently available. In concentrating on the individual course interactions, institutions have often neglected the fuller academic resource supports necessary to mount full-service web-based degree programmes.

Librarians are faced with the challenge of linking students from widely varying backgrounds to information sources and drawing them into patterns of regular library use. By creating a positive climate, the school library can provide English as a Second Language (ESL) students with a place for learning, sharing, and personal growth. The ESL students were introduced to the library at a time when no other classes were there. Each student was given a diagram of the library, then walked through each area beginning at the entrance. Hands-on activities were provided, such as practice in using the copy machine. Thereafter, students returned to the library on an individual basis, or in pairs, with a specific request to the librarian; at this time, individual explanations and demonstrations were given of the various areas and their uses. Eventually, students were sent to the librarian with individual assignments. By this time, students were familiar with the library staff and did not hesitate to approach them for help. Students were encouraged to use the library before school, after school, and during study hall periods.

As a result, the ESL students found the library to be a safe and welcoming place and became frequent users. To draw ESL students into a pattern of regular library use, the library established a collection of reading materials in their first languages. To meet the full range of interests and reading abilities, collections of fiction and non-fiction books in Spanish, Arabic, and Portuguese were borrowed for extended periods through Interlibrary Loan. With school library funds, a small collection of Portuguese books, a weekly Portuguese newspaper, a Spanish newspaper, and foreign language dictionaries were purchased. Spanish magazines were contributed by the Spanish language teacher. High-interest, low-reading-level paperbacks in English were borrowed from a local public library's literacy collection. At the request of the ESL teacher, these books were housed in the ESL classroom for easy access during classroom times. A listening station with a cassette player and headphone and a collection of read-along books in English were made available in the library conference room. Most books were classics that are required reading for high school students. In addition, a collection of wordless books was borrowed from several public libraries.

Many elementary school ESL teachers report multiple uses of these books, including promotion of oral language and conversation skills, development of sequence and prediction skills, and development of vocabulary skills. For all students, but especially for ESL students, the optimal learning process involves connecting new ideas with old knowledge. To provide materials required for this, the librarian introduced the use of advanced organizers, an essential instructional strategy proposed by Ausubel to enhance classroom learning. That the information-processing system of humans is a set of ideas that provides anchors for new information or ideas, that in turn provides a storehouse when new meanings are acquired. Central to enhancing the learning process for students with language needs is the technique of building learning upon prior learning and knowledge.

Based on this view of how learners process information, and the realization that much of the material to be learned by ESL students is completely new and unrelated to anything they know, the librarian created opportunities for ESL students to gain essential prior knowledge through the use of advance organizers. Collaboration between the librarian and the ESL teacher resulted in a list of key themes and subject areas related to the ESL text and curriculum.

Appropriate materials were acquired, borrowed, and collected by the librarian for use in both the media center and in the ESL classroom. Because this strategy relies heavily on visuals and pictorial materials, a picture file was developed for advance organizers. To collect materials suitable for use as advance organizers, the librarian used references for collecting visuals with pictures of all kinds, especially designed for second language learners, a directory of resource organizations, and various bibliographies.

## Multicultural Education as a Transformational Process

Multicultural education is a movement in schools to promote awareness, mutual appreciation, and harmony among people of different cultural groups—usually with the ultimate goal of achieving social justice and social cohesion. It came into being where fair-minded people sought ways to respond constructively to the challenge of members of different cultural groups sharing the same society. Although social action for justice may begin in other domains— laws and policies, hiring practices, housing, or access to health care, for example—sooner or later, schools must be involved in the effort. That is because progress in social arrangements ultimately requires that citizens adopt new attitudes, which in turn need new knowledge and experiences. Teachers who approach multicultural education often begin with the formal curriculum—with the content that is taught. Some, however, attempt to change the implicit aspects of schooling, too—to make aspects of schooling like power-sharing and interaction among students more supportive of students from all cultural groups and ultimately of the goal of social change.

In the most straightforward of venues, multicultural education is limited to discussions of school curriculum. From a practical standpoint, this translates into using materials such as children's books, or projects such as oral histories, to increase awareness and understanding of the various cultural perspectives of the students in the school or classroom. The idea is that the content connects to the child and hence, each child will see himself or herself reflected in the daily curriculum and studies that take place in the classroom. Further, that the class will see itself as a collective made up of different experiences, all of which are equally important and valid, and by doing so will increase the understanding of each child of the other. In other contexts, such as the political arena, multicultural education takes on a much broader scope and has been defined as "any set of processes by which schools work with rather than against oppressed groups."

The most inclusive definitions suggest that multicultural education is a transformational process that permeates and impacts every aspect of the operation of an educational system, including government policy, staffing, curriculum, disciplinary policy, student involvement, parent and community involvement, pedagogy, assessment, and funding. One of the underlying premises of multicultural education as transformation is "that as schools go so goes the nation," At the practical level, multicultural education then becomes a venue for social and political reform.

Discussions of oppression, social inequality, power dynamics, race and ethnicity, as well as the role of the dominant culture, in the shaping of society's basic assumption about what constitutes school knowledge, appropriate social behavior, and national identity, is all part of the multicultural education discourse. Regardless of where practice comes down on the definitional continuum, researchers, architects, and practitioners of multicultural education hold certain goals and assumptions in common. Multicultural education assumes that pluralism is a good thing and that race, ethnicity, cultural and social class are all salient parts of a pluralistic society. Participation in a variety of ethnic experiences ultimately enriches one's understanding of the human experience and leads to a more fulfilling life. A central goal of multicultural education is to help individuals live more productively in a pluralistic society. This is accomplished in two ways:

— Individuals gain a greater understanding of themselves by seeing themselves through the lens of other cultures.

— Individuals gain the necessary skills, knowledge, and attitudes needed to function within their ethnic culture and within and across other ethnic cultures.

Multicultural education is premised on the need for accuracy. In order for individuals to get a true picture of historical and social events, which have shaped national identity, they need to listen to multiple voices and understand multiple perspectives. It is not a matter of leaving out one version of events in favor of another; rather it is about re-envisioning history using an inclusive model that more accurately portrays events as they happened. Multicultural education is a commitment to helping all students master the essential academic and social skills to become knowledgeable, caring, and active citizens in an increasingly polarized and troubled world.

Regardless of how individuals view the multicultural education movement, there are some general models and specific areas of research that offer educators and policy makers a road map for program development. The two most often cited general modes are offered by Banks and by Sleeter and Gran. These models differ from one another but are not mutually exclusive. Other researchers such as Nieto, Delpit, and Ladson-Billings focus on particular areas of multicultural program development and offer suggestions relating to pedagogy, curriculum, and structure. Ladson-Billings, for example, focuses on the specifics of successful literacy education for African American students. Delpit is concerned with power relations in a classroom that can exist when minority children are taught by teachers of the dominant culture. Nieto is focused on institutional reform and student achievement.

When discussing theoretical models, how they actually look and operate in a classroom or school is often left out of the conversation. In that regard, Burnett suggests a third model that combines Banks, Sleeter, current research with an overview of actual programs as they are currently underway in the United States. Burnett's typology is particularly useful in that it reflects the translation of theory into practice and divides programs into three general categories according to program emphasis.

a) *Content-oriented programs*: Content-oriented programs are the most easily recognizable and hence the most common form of multicultural education. These are committed to the inclusion of material that reflects the cultural make-up of the class or the school. The primary goal of these programs is to make students more knowledgeable about cultures within their schools or their communities. These programs come in various levels of engagement and infusion of the curriculum. In its simplest form, " this type of program gives a multicultural patina to the standard curriculum" by incorporating a few readings and the celebration of heroes and holidays of diverse groups. It gives only a cursory nod to multicultural education by focusing solely on "heroes and holiday." Students would read books, do projects, and learn about a variety of holidays but through the lens of the standard canon. At this stage, multicultural education is an add-on or tangential to current curriculum without changing the actual focus. More sophisticated and complex programs, however, set out to actually transform the curriculum. These programs have three goals:

— to develop multicultural content across the disciplines

— to incorporate a variety of different viewpoints and perspectives in the curriculum

— to transform the canon, ultimately developing a new paradigm for the curriculum.

b) Student-oriented programs: Student-oriented programs address the academic and learning needs of carefully defined groups of students, most specifically minority students. The goal of these programs is often to raise the academic achievement of these groups. Research in learning styles, language use and development, etc. often forms the basis of these programs. Since the goal of student-oriented programs is to improve the academic success of specific groups and thereby make it possible for them to enter the mainstream, they are often seen as compensatory in nature. Further, there is no particular guarantee that student-oriented programs will be done in conjunction with content oriented programs. In fact, it is entirely possible to have one without the other. Again Banks suggests four broad program categories:

— programs that use research into culturally-based learning styles in order to match teaching styles to a specific group of students

— bi-lingual education or language/cultural immersion

— special math and science programs for groups, such as females and minorities that are seen as underachieving in these areas.

— Language programs and cultural programs specific to minority group

c) *Socially-oriented programs*: Socially-oriented programs are generally the most inclusive and broad-based. They are also often controversial and as a consequence less common. Programs such as these attempt to reform "both the schooling and the cultural and political contexts of schooling". The over-arching goal of socially-oriented programs is to increase cultural and racial tolerance and reduce bias as well as rearrange the social structure to reinforce and support this new paradigm. In order to accomplish this, socially-oriented programs have a number of distinguishing characteristics:

— They seek to revise and transform the curriculum to create a new canon that is reflective of the current society.

— They seek to use current educational research to discover new ways to engage students in the educational enterprise in order that they may be academically successful, regardless of ethnicity and class.

— They use the instruments and strategies of social activism and community organization to accomplish these goals.

— They focus on the outcome of preparing students to be socially – active citizens and agents of change.

Socially-oriented programs use a variety of approaches borrowed from disciplines as diverse as philosophy, ecology, and psychology. Some programs emphasize critical thinking and critical discourse, collaborative learning and multilingualism. Other programs focus on the use of the ecological model to enhance understanding of social structures and the diffusion of change, still other programs focus on the nature of inclusion and consensus and how best to translate those concepts into practice, not only at the classroom level but at the school and community level as well.

## Need of a Multicultural Approach

There is a danger in multicultural education programming of letting the political rhetoric and the academic research agenda overshadow the benefits of designing and implementing interesting and lively opportunities for children to learn. In fact, the reasons to use a multicultural approach in schools are simple and compelling.

— A multicultural approach makes learning more interesting and relevant to children's lives.

— A multicultural approach gives all students a forum in which to share information about who they are, how they live, what is important to them and their families.

— A multicultural approach gives students another lens through which to view history and society.

— A multicultural approach encourages tolerance and respect and supports notions of social reform and community cohesion.

# 4

# Child Education: Challenges

In school, children have to learn many different things. Some children seem to learn quickly; others are slower. In certain subjects, child may do better than others. We can group children's difficulties into two broad types. Those which rise from bodily impairments and those which come from deprivation. Some children may be disadvantaged because of combination of disadvantages. In addition, any child can experience barriers to learning during a period of time. These temporary difficulties may occur because, for example, the child is worried about problems at home; she has not slept properly because her sister or brother is ill and crying all the night; she has been working a lot in the fields and is too tired to concentrate on learning, etc. Although these difficulties will probably be overcome as time goes by, it is important that the teacher is sensitive and supportive, and helps the child to catch up whatever she has missed during this period.

Children who have physical, sensory or intellectual impairments can experience many difficulties in learning and participating in community life. For example, a child may have lost a limb as the result of accident; have wasted legs following polio or been born with deformed limbs because of cerebral palsy. Often they are called 'disabled' in that they are unable to walk or to climb stairs. But more importantly this disability often holds the child back in various ways. As the child cannot move around the house or neighbourhood as other children do, then:

— his opportunities to join in community life are also fewer –he cannot go as easily to market or family gatherings.

— she may be ashamed of her body; have lack of confidence and try to avoid playing with other children.

As you read back over the list of consequences; you will see that it is not the impairment that should concern teachers or how it was caused, but rather it is reducing the consequences that the impairment brings to the child's life and the barriers that it presents to children's learning.

Some people think that the solution to all these problems is to remove the impairment so that the child can walk again. Medical cures are often sought. Perhaps the doctors could operate on their legs "or "special exercises could be prescribed to make their legs work normally ". These can certainly help with some people but what if they don't work or these options are not available to children and families where you live.

There are plenty of things that can be done to reduce the negative consequences even though we cannot cure the impairment. Here are some ideas –perhaps you will be able to add others.

— We can teach the person to walk using crutches or sticks.

— We can get the person a wheelchair.

— We can make sure that there are no steps up to buildings.

— We adapt the toilet so that the person can move from wheelchair on to it.

— We make sure that his brothers and sisters play with the child.

This way of thinking places a responsibility on educators and the community. If we fail to do any of the things listed then the children will be more disabled. Hence it is not the impairment that holds back the person but the way in which society treats the person. That is why some people prefer to be called 'disabled persons' because they feel that society, and the environment in which they live, has disabled them. Throughout the world this social view of disability is becoming more accepted.

## Disabilities of Children

All children learn through their interactions with other people –parents, siblings and peers –and through the experiences gained in the various environments in their lives – home, neighbourhood and school. This is just as true for children with impairments. But this is often forgotten as these children were seen as 'different'. Indeed their lack of learning or slow development was put down to their impairment rather than to the restrictions they experienced in interacting with others and to participating in different environments.

Many of the disabling effects of impairments can be reduced if children have the opportunity;

— to interact with peers and adults in their community

— to experience a range of environments which minimise the impact of their impairment, such as buildings that have no steps

— to be taught by parents and teachers who help them to learn new skills.

— Sometimes the social view of disability is presented as an alternative to the 'medical view' of disability.

This seeks to identify the cause of the disability through tests and then tries to fix the impairment through the use of surgery, drugs or therapy. Both viewpoints are valid and both are needed. But too often only the medical view is considered and when it fails or is not available, people give up.

The biggest danger with the medical view is that the 'problem' is seen solely as being with the child. That's why children with impairments were excluded from ordinary schools and sent to special schools for children with the same disability – if they were available. The belief was that they required special 'treatments' because of their impairments.

But as we have explained, disabilities result not from impartments but from lack of opportunities, participation and education. There is a great deal that parents and teachers can do to reduce the disabilities that come from impairments. Children can have different impairments – problems in seeing and hearing; physical impairments or conditions such as epilepsy (fits) and intellectual impairments which affect their thinking.

Medical science has found the causes of many of the impairments. Some result from genetic damage when the baby is conceived; some come from infections while the baby is in the womb; and a few may happen as the child is being born. Childhood illnesses and accidents can also result in bodily impairments.

However we want you to think about the disabilities which can result from impairments such as hearing loss, vision problems, epilepsy, intellectual disability and so on. You should do this in the same way as was done above for the physical impairment.

1. Select an impairment that you are familiar with. Perhaps someone in your family or among friends and neighbours has it, or you may have taught a child with the impairment.

2. Note down the disabilities you have noticed that come from having that impairment; that is the things that the person may be unable to do because of the impairment.

3. Then list some ideas that parents, teachers and others in the community could do to lessen the disabling effects of that impairment.

4. Do this for two different impairments.

5. Then answer the two questions at the bottom of the page.

All children have basic needs –for love and affection, security, nutritious food, healthy environment and shelter. If any of these are missing or in short supply, then the child's growth and development may be held back. Put simply, their ability to learn is reduced. Hence teachers and schools must try to ensure that their pupils are not held back because their basic needs re not being met.

The basic needs of many children with disabilities are not met. They may not be given enough food because they do not demand it; their poor health is not attended to as it is presumed to be associated with their impairment or they are not shown the same love and affection because they are different. How do we remove deprivations in the child's environment? The answers are obvious –good food, secure shelter, safe water, good health care and loving careers. Schools alone cannot solve these problems but neither can they leave them to other people to solve.

Germs that get into the child's mouth with food and water cause more than half of all illnesses and deaths among young children. In communities without latrines, without safe drinking water and without safe refuse disposal, it is very difficult for families to prevent the spread of germs.

It is therefore vital for the government to support communities by providing –as a minimum – the materials and technical advice needed to construct latrines and improve drinking water supplies. Information campaigns are needed and schools can play a key role in this.

Children need to be immunised against diseases that cause disabilities, such as measles, polio and whooping cough. Protective actions need to be taken wherever malaria is common. The dangers to health from drugs, sexually transmitted diseases and HIV/AIDS need to be communicated to families and young people. Schools should cooperate with health education campaigns running in their locality.

In affluent countries children's emotional needs may not be responded to even though their physical needs are well met. If the children's emotional needs are not met, their capacity to learn will be impaired.

All children need a close, sensitive and loving relationship with the adult or adults who care for them. It is the basis for the development of the child's sense of security, confidence and the ability to cope well with other people and the world at large. Children gain a feeling of security when careers are consistent in their actions and words. They also learn what is expected in human relationships, and they develop clear sense of what is right and wrong.

Appropriate rules and limitations should be clearly communicated and explained to the child. Careers need to be consistent in their expectations of how the child should behave. Anger and violence in the child's family can be damaging to the child's inner development. However, it is also important that the child learns to express anger and frustration in an appropriate manner.

The mind of child, as well as the body, needs help to grow. The three most important 'foods' for the growth of the mind are language, play and love. From his earliest months, a child needs to be bathed in words, cuddled, smiled at, listened to, and encouraged to respond by noise and movement. All children need to interact with other people. They need people to touch, talk to, laugh with, smile at, respond to and get responses from. Lack of attention makes a child unhappy. A neglected child loses interest in life, can have less appetite, and may fail to grow normally in mind or body.

Children learn by doing. So as the child grows, he or she needs freedom to explore and to play. Play is not pointless. It is one of the most essential parts of growing up. It helps to develop mental, social and physical skills – including talking and walking. It helps children grow in curiosity, competence and confidence. It digs the foundations for schoolwork and for learning the skills necessary in later life.

Play does not always mean solving problems or achieving aims set by adults. The child's own play alone or with other children is just as important. Parents and careers need to encourage play by providing materials and ideas. Play materials do not have to be expensive. Empty boxes or household objects are as good as expensive toys. Imaginative play, for example when children pretend to be adults, is very important to a child's development.

Children need help to develop creativity. They need to be challenged to and solutions to problems and decide which solutions are best. The child needs to put his or her ideas and decisions into practice and see what happens – in safety. Singing songs and learning rhymes, drawing pictures and reading stories aloud help the child's mind grow and prepares the way for learning to read and write. All children learn by participating in daily routines of the family and household work. Children with special needs re able to contribute, too, if the family creatively finds ways to facilitate it and communicate the social meanings of the daily life. For healthy growth, all children need praise and recognition for their efforts.

In all countries of the world, people with disabilities have often been treated as 'less than human' and of little value to society. Today that attitude is being replaced with a respect for these persons. The United Nations

Declaration on the Rights of Disabled Persons (1975) states:

> Disabled persons have the inherent right to respect for their human dignity. Disabled persons whatever the origin, nature and seriousness of their handicaps and disabilities have the same fundamental rights as their fellow citizens of the same age, which implies first and foremost the right to enjoy a decent life, as normal and as full as possible. (Article 3).

Likewise, the Governments of the world have agreed that the same rights apply to all children irrespective of their impairments or environments. Hence the Convention on the Rights of the Child states that;

> Recognising the special needs of a disabled child, assistance....shall be provided to ensure that the disabled child has effective access to and receives education conducive...to the child achieving the fullest possible social integration and individual development (Article 23).

Both these declarations make clear how important it is for all especially to have the opportunity to grow into their culture, absorb its values and beliefs and contribute to its development. This is essential if children are to develop sense of identity and sense of belonging. The family, schools and the community activities are society's primary means of doing this. But this can only happen if they are socially included as active participants in their family and community. These same principles apply to other marginalised groups in societies; such as travelling peoples, ethnic minorities and refugees. The wellbeing of their children is threatened if they are denied opportunities to socially integrate in their communities and wider society.

The United Nations General Assembly adopted the Standard Rules on the Equalization of Opportunities for Persons with Disabilities in 1993. Rule 6 states;

> States should recognise the principle of equal primary, secondary and tertiary educational opportunities for their children, youth and adults with disabilities, in integrated settings. They should ensure that the education of persons with disabilities is an integral part of the education system.

UNESCO (the United Nations Educational, Scientific and Cultural Organisation) issued the 'Salamanca Statement and Framework for Action', adopted at the World Conference on Special Needs Education in 1994. This spelt out the implications of these statements of rights. It states;

- Every child has a fundamental right to education and must be given the opportunity to achieve and maintain an acceptable level of learning.
- Educational systems should be designed and educational programmes implemented to take into account the wide diversity of characteristics and needs. Those with special educational needs must have access to regular school.
- Regular schools with this inclusive orientation are the most effective means of
  - combating discriminatory attitudes,
  - creating welcoming communities, building an inclusive society and
  - achieving education for all.

— Moreover ordinary schools provide an effective education to the majority of children and improve the efficiency and ultimately the cost-effectiveness of the entire education system.

The slogan Education for All means just that; all children including those who have impairments or come from marginalised groups within society. In the past, separate schools for 'different' children was the favoured solution in many countries. Experience has taught us that this approach can mean that many children in less affluent countries and areas get no education at all! Among the reasons are;

— Special schools are a high cost option which many poorer countries cannot afford.

— They tend to be located in urban centres and serve more affluent families.

— The expertise of specialist teachers is not shared with regular teachers.

— Equally the value of special schools is questioned in more affluent countries for these and other reasons.

— Inclusive schools provide children with more educational and social opportunities.

— Parents increasingly opt to send their children to ordinary schools; some parents see special schools as a form of discrimination.

— Disabled activists have been critical of the education they received in special schools.

However, the Salamanca Statement and Framework for Action referred to above does recognise that certain children may be best taught in special classes or schools because of their particular needs in communication;

namely those who are deaf or, deaf-blind. However, there are also examples from many countries, where deaf children are also successfully included in ordinary schools. What do these statements of rights mean for teachers and schools? We can summarise the position as follows;

— All children have a right to education.

— This should happen as far as possible in ordinary schools –preprimary, primary and secondary.

— Certain children because of their impairments or through deprivation may require extra assistance.

— Teachers and schools need to adapt their ways of working to meet the children's needs.

— This will result in an improved and more cost-effective education system as well as benefiting all children and their families.

Statements of rights and government policies may set aims but it is individual teachers who can make inclusive education a success or a failure. They too can hold negative attitudes just as others do in society. Often their fears and prejudices are based on a lack of contact with people who are disabled or who have disadvantaged backgrounds. When they meet and get to know these people their attitudes can change. Read the views of teachers in Lesotho, a country in southern Africa, and in Guyana, in South America. As you have read, four out of five teachers report benefits to having children with disabilities in their school. Similar results have been found in other countries. But teachers still had their problems! Among the most commonly mentioned problems by these teachers were the following.

— Pupil not coping with reading, writing, number work

— Pupils are slower to learn and understand

— Behaviour disrupts class

— Communicating with the pupil; not following instructions

— Pupils needs more time and attention from the teacher

— Class/school environment not suitable

— Pupil has poor attention /concentration

— Toileting

— Teacher not equipped to deal with the pupil

— The teachers might have tried to solve these problems by excluding these children from their class or school.

— The teachers knew that it would mean the pupils are denied their right to education and they accepted the challenge of developing their skills at supporting all children to learn.

The teachers see their school as a welcoming place for all children. They believe each child should fully develop their abilities; be entiated learning possibilities and be supported in a positive learning environment. The school has developed a local curriculum and published their own curriculum materials in mathematics and Hungarian. The books present graded tasks which allow students to work at their own level and pace, but with similar content. These materials has helped all students to learn better.

### *Common Impairments*

With some children, their impairments are obvious. If they are thin and underweight, they could be malnourished. Likewise you will quickly spot any physical deformity or an inability to control their hand and arm movements. In these instances, the action needed to help the child at school is clear. For example You may have noted the need to use classrooms on ground level for these children; installing ramps if there are steps into the classroom ; moving desks around to accommodate the chair and improving access to toilets. Of course all these things make it easier for everyone to move around the school –including teachers who may have difficulties walking! Children with physical disabilities do not usually have any specific learning needs – they just need to have and access to schools and classrooms, although sometimes they may need some assistive devices to help them to write and to read. However some impairments are not so easily seen. It is presumed the child has no problem and hence teachers and schools may not adapt their ways of working.

Families and teachers can miss children with difficulties in hearing; difficulties in seeing and problems in learning. Along with physical disabilities, these are the impairments that teachers in ordinary schools are most likely to come across.

— Some children have more than one impairment.

— Most of these impairments should be identified when the child first comes to school.

— It is important for teachers to identify the child's abilities as well as their disabilities.

— Teachers should share information about the children with impairments especially when they move on from their class. Sometimes the impairments worsen as children grow older and other children can experience problems when they are older. Teachers in secondary schools also need to be alert to these conditions.

— And most important of all; late identification and poor teaching in the early years will make the child's difficulties more severe.

*Hearing impairments*

We use the term 'hearing impaired' but other terms are 'hard of hearing' or 'deafness'. Often we presume that children can hear when in fact they might have difficulties hearing. Children cannot tell us they have problems in hearing because they may not know what it is like to hear properly.

Mild hearing losses are much more common in school populations than profound hearing loss. Remember too, that some hearing problems come and go. If a child is prone to head colds or recurrent ear infections, their hearing can also be affected.

If a student does not pay attention in class it is possible that he or she cannot hear what is being said or the sounds the child hears may be distorted. Due to these reasons the child either tunes out what the teacher says or does not make an effort to listen or attend. Very rarely a student may be exceptionally attentive by playing very close attention in an attempt to determine what is being said.

— *Poor speech development*: Immature, unusual or distorted speech may be due to hearing loss. Or the child talks in very loud or soft voice.

— *Difficulty in following instructions;* A child who has unusual difficulty in following oral instruction can have a possible hearing impairment.

  — The child may respond better to tasks assigned when the teacher is relatively close to him and her, or to written tasks rather than ones that require an oral response.

  — The student may turn or cock head to one side to hear better.

  — Hearing problems can cause the child to watch what other students are doing before starting his/her work or looking at classmates or teachers for clues.

  — A child may have difficulty in hearing text read by others or the child may request his peers or teachers to speak louder.

  — Sometimes the child may give an inappropriate answer to question asked or fail to answer.

  — Children with a hearing loss prefer to work in small groups, sit in a relatively quiet area of the classroom or in the front row.

  — The student may be shy or withdrawn or appear to be stubborn and disobedient as a reaction to his hearing loss.

  — The student may be reluctant to participate in oral activities, may fail to laugh at jokes or understand humour.

— The student may tend to isolate herself/himself from social activities.

— The student may interpret facial expressions, body movements and contextual information rather than spoken language and thus sometimes make false conclusions.

— The student may complain of frequent earaches, colds, sore throat or recurrent tonsillitis.

— The student may have some discharge from the ears.

Some children are born with impaired hearing; others may lose their hearing later on. We have listed the various causes of hearing impairment as this can also alert you to children who may have problems with hearing. The more common causes are;

— Hereditary (hearing impairment occur in certain families, although the child's parents may not be hearing impaired. This happens more with boys than girls and is more common in affluent countries.)

— The mother had German measles during early pregnancy

— Lack of iodine in mother's diet

— Prematurity (baby born early and small)

— Ear infections, especially long lasting, repeated infections with pus

— Excessive earwax that blocks the ear canal

— Meningitis (an infection of the brain)

— Cerebral malaria and overdoses of medicines used in its treatment However, in one out of three cases the cause of the hearing impairment is not known.

*Classroom adaptations*

— The child should be seated as close as possible to the teachers.

— The teachers must make sure to stand or sit facing the pupil. Do not cover your face with book when reading; or talk when writing on the chalkboard.

_ Make sure light does not come from behind you, as your face would be in shadow. Work in good light so that the child can see your face, hands or lips.

_ Some pupils benefit from seeing both the teacher and their classmates at the same time. They can learn from seeing other pupils responding to the teacher. So position the child in class accordingly or arrange the desks in such a way that it is possible for children to see each other's faces.

— Try to minimise classroom noises. Use a room that is in a quieter part of the school.

*Teaching strategies*

— If a hearing aid has been prescribed for the child make sure it is worn; that it is switched on and that the batteries are good.

— Clearly and loudly but without shouting and exaggerating.

— Use simple words and sentences along with gestures or pictures to help the child understand what you are saying.

— Children with hearing impairments learn more from seeing rather than hearing although teachers should use both. Show them what you expect them to do. Use pictorial material or symbol cards.

— Pair the pupil with hearing student. The partner can help and the correct page; repeat your instructions and so on.

— Encourage the pupil with hearing impairment to watch and listen to other pupils as they answer your questions. If they cannot see other pupils and hear their responses, you may repeat what they said as you face the pupil with the hearing impairment.

— Chĕck with the pupil that he or she understands what she is expected to do.

— Children with hearing impairments might find group situations more difficult because of all the talking going on at the same time by different people. Teachers can use these times to give facetoface instruction to a pupil with hearing impairments.

— If the child's speech is not clear, take time to listen to what the child is trying to tell you. Help him ·to use the correct words and grammar but praise for their efforts at talking.

With children who are deaf – those with very little hearing –the main means of communication has to be through sign language; lip reading or reading and writing can be used as additional means of communication. All of the above suggestions apply with deaf children but you should also consider the following;

— Teachers need to take classes in learning the sign language that is used by deaf people in their country. Adult deaf persons, who are trained as sign language instructors, are often the best teachers.

— Young children quickly learn to sign even when their teacher or parents are not very good at it. The more you practice signing the better you become.

— Teachers can recap the lesson through signs for their deaf students or alternate spoken and sign language during the lessons.

— It may be possible to arrange for an interpreter/ teachers of sign language to come regularly to the school. Deaf adults can be used as volunteers in the class to support the deaf child and facilitate communication between the child, the teacher and the classmates.

— As children's language skills develop, introduce reading as this offers a most important medium of learning for the child and in communicating with others.

— Try to ensure that the deaf student receives written copies of lessons from you or her peers. Try to offer books and written material as often as possible.

— In many countries, special units have been set up for deaf children in ordinary schools, usually in urban areas. Deaf adults may be employed as teachers and classroom assistants. Here pupils are taught through sign language and they can use it to communicate easily with one another. Equally they have opportunities to socialise with all other pupils and join them for some classes.

— The child can be referred to health worker or doctor for an ear examination. She should be able to clear infections and excess wax.

— The child's hearing can be tested by an audiologist. He will determine precisely the degree and type of hearing loss experienced by the child. Hearing aids may be prescribed. These amplify the sound for the child but they are not suitable for certain types of hearing difficulties. Also they can be expensive to purchase and maintain as they require batteries. Audiology services are usually provided in hospitals, sometimes in public or private health care clinics and mobile hearing screening clinics. Enquire from your health care professionals. Although it is important that the child's hearing is tested, you can immediately use some of the above advise when you suspect hearing impairment. You can also and out from the child the difficulties she experiences in hearing, what is said in the classroom and what makes it easier for her to hear.

*Visual Impairments*

Various terms are used to describe differing degrees and types of visual impairment such as low vision, partial sight and blindness. Many children's problems are easily corrected with glasses once the problem is identified but some will have more marked impairments. Some of the warning signs are easily observed but it is possible for other problems to go unnoticed.

— *Physical indictors*: There may be red eyes, crusts on lids among the eye lashes, recurring styes or swollen eyelids, watery eyes or discharge, crossed eye, eyes that do not appear straight, pupils of uneven size, eyes that have excessive and drooping eyelids.

— The student rubs eyes often or while doing close visual work.

— The student shuts or covers one eye when he has difficulty seeing with that eye or tilts the head or thrusts the head forward.

— Unusual facial behaviours; A student shows unusual amount of squinting, blinking, frowning, or facial distortion while reading or doing other close work.

— Unable to locate and pick up a small object.

— Light sensitivity or difficulty; A student may show unusual sensitivity to bright light by shutting their eyes or squinting. He may have a difficulty in seeing in dim light or inability to see after dark.

— Difficulty with reading; An unusual difficulty with reading or when working that requires bringing the book or object close to the eyes. But he may do very well in oral or spoken directions and tasks.

— The pupil may have difficulty with written work; like not being able to stay on the line or write within the spaces.

— Difficulty with distance vision may result in the pupil avoiding the playground, or avoiding all gross motor activity. Such student may prefer reading or other academic activity.

The more common causes are:

— Infectious diseases contracted by the mother during the first few months of pregnancy

— Infectious diseases contracted by the child, e. g. measles or chicken pox

— Maternal or childhood malnutrition. Eating yellow and green fruits and vegetables helps to protect the eyes.

  — Eye infections

  — Injuries to the eye

- — Tumours affecting nerve for sight
- — Brain damage
- — Xerophtalmia, i. e. nutritional blindness as a result of insufficient Vitamin A in the diet
- — River blindness caused by bathing in infected water

*Classroom adaptations*

- — Find out from the child where is the best place for her to see the chalkboard, for example when seated at the front of the class.
- — The light should not reflect on the board and you should ensure that the chalk appears clearly on the board.
- — If the child's eyes are sensitive to the light, move him way from the window. Have him wear peaked hat to shade his eyes or give him cardboard screen to use for shade when reading and writing.
- — Ensure the child knows her way around the school and the classroom. Teachers and sighted pupils should lead her by walking in front with the visually impaired pupil slightly behind and to one side; holding on to the guide's elbow. Warn them of obstacles such as steps and narrow doorways.

*Teaching strategies*

- — Use large writing on the chalkboard or visual aids. The use of coloured chalks is recommended. Let the children come close to the board or teaching aids so that they can see more easily.
- — Read aloud what is written on the blackboard.

— Prepare teaching aids that children can read more easily such as large print materials. Other children in the class could help prepare these. Or they can be produced by enlarging images on photocopies or using larger font sizes on computer printouts. This can also help children who have difficulties in reading.

— Children may have difficulty seeing the lines on writing paper. They can be given paper with thicker lines drawn on it.

— Some children will benefit from using magnifying aids. Two types are available. Ones that enlarge the whole page or line magnifiers, which re useful aid to reading.

— Encourage the children to use a pointer or their finger when reading. Cover the rest of the page with paper except for the paragraph the child is reading. Use a bookstand to avoid reflection.

— Children with poor vision need to learn through touch as well as through hearing. They should be given a chance to handle objects.

— Pair the pupil with a seeing classmate who can assist her to organise their work. The partner can help and the correct page; repeat your instructions and so on.

— Use verbal praise or touch to give the child encouragement.

— Use the name of the pupils during class discussions so that the child knows who is talking.

— Computers offer particular support to students with vision impairments and blindness. Students can print out a large print copy, read text on the screen using screen enlargement software, listen to the text on a voice synthesiser or convert it into Braille.

— Make an abacus available to the child in maths lessons.

— Lessons can be taped using a cassette recorder for later playback at home or as revision. Students who experience difficulties in writing can also provide information on audiotape.

### *Teaching strategies for blind children*

Blind children have little or no useful vision; they are only able to make out light and dark. Many of the suggestions above apply to these children too but there are others you also need to consider.

— *Blind children should learn Braille.* This gives them means of reading and writing. Perkins Braillers are available across all countries. Braille can be produced directly on a Braille embosser. Also Braille texts can be produced from computer textile format and printed out using a Braille printer. Details will be available from your national association for the blind. They will help you to find teachers of Braille. Once children can use Braille they can learn alongside sighted children.

— *Tactile images can be drawn on Braille* paper using special mat and stylus which produces a relief image that can be felt. Similar images can be produced using locally available materials such as string, sand, sticks and seeds. Teachers can enlist the help of sighted children in producing teaching aids. These aids help other children, too.

— Likewise an abacus will help all children in maths lessons.

— Blind children need to learn to orientate their bodies and to move confidently. Physical activities and group games will provide good practice. At first children will need to be moved through the activity in order to understand what they are to do.

— Blind children should be encouraged to walk independently around the school using a cane. It should be the same length as the distance from the ground up to halfway between the person's shoulder and waist. A cane that is too short will force the user to bend over when walking. Ideally they should receive training from specialists. Your national association for the blind should be able to advise. Do not remove obstacles all the time, as children have to be trained to move around them.

— Daily living skills such as cooking pose particular challenges for blind persons. However children need to acquire these skills in a graded manner, starting with low risk activities before moving on to activities in which there is a risk of burning themselves.

— The child can be referred to health worker or doctor to clear infections or to have their health checked.

— The child's vision can be tested by opticians. Glasses may be prescribed and the child should be encouraged to wear them.

*Intellectual disability*

Many of the suggested adjustments and strategies can facilitate learning of all children in the class. By considering how you can reduce the barriers to learning experienced by a blind child, you will improve your teaching for all children. Of all the disabilities this is the most common. Other terms are often used to describe this disability; for example, developmental disability, mental retardation, mental handicap or severe learning difficulties. This disability affects all aspects of a child's development. They are slower to develop physically, acquire language, learn to look after themselves and in mastering academic skills. However they are not mentally ill. That term is used when healthy people develop an illness that affects their moods, emotions and behaviours. With appropriate treatment they can be cured.

With some children their intellectual impairment is obvious at birth, or soon after. But with many others, it will not be identified until the child starts school although the warning signs are often present from young age. Some children might have very severe disabilities and may have additional impairments such as epilepsy, vision and hearing problems. They are sometimes referred to as profoundly or multiply disabled children.

However many more children are affected only mildly or moderately –a rough estimate is two in one hundred. With these children there be may no physical reason for their disability. The signs have been grouped into six areas. Children who show signs in all these areas are more likely to have an intellectual disability. Problems that occur in one area but not in another, may be indicative of a specific learning difficulty related to reading, writing or maths, for example.

The best yardstick is the ages which children in that community usually attain these skills. Even so, the guidelines should be used cautiously as there is much variation in children's development. Some children develop naturally slower than others without having an intellectual disability. Deprivation can cause this kind of slower development. Living in a multilingual community can also slow down child's language development, as she is learning several languages at the same time. Remember too that children may develop intellectual disability later in life having acquired these milestones. This can be the result of head injury or severe deprivation.

*Reading and writing*

By five years of age or after one year at school, the child

— has difficulty copying shapes such as circles and squares

— has problems doing simple jigsaws and form boards

— mixes up letters such as d and b

— has difficulty sequencing letters and words on

— ash cards

— cannot recall

— five numbers or words in the correct order immediately after they are spoken.

Intellectual disabilities have many different causes. They can be grouped into five types;

— *Genetic damage:* This is present at conception. Down Syndrome is an example of a genetic fault.

— *Damage in womb:* Infections in the mother can damage the developing baby. Rubella or German measles is a common example. The HIV virus can also damage growing brains.

— *Damage at birth or soon after:* Oxygen deprivation, low birth weight and premature births, and jaundice can all result in intellectual disabilities.

— *Accidents and illnesses:* Damage to the brain from falls or accidents can result in intellectual disabilities as can infections such as cerebral malaria and meningitis, repeated fits and malnutrition.

— *Social causes:* Children who are extremely deprived of love and affection and stimulation can also experience in extreme cases intellectual disabilities. However with sizeable numbers of children – upwards of one-third –no cause can be found for their disability. Remember that the same cause can produce very different effects in children. For example, child born with Down Syndrome may grow and develop much like any other child whereas others with the same genetic damage are markedly disabled. Beware of expecting too little from the child because of the label given to their disability. Children need to be offered materials and experiences that will challenge them.

*Classroom adaptations*

Teachers who have experience of teaching children with intellectual disability and learning difficulties in their class recommend:

— Reduce distractions – keep the desk clear.

— With children who are inclined to run around, seat them by the wall with bigger children beside them. You can also assign them tasks that allow them to move around so that this moving does not become disruptive, such as handing out papers, notebooks and materials.

— Try to recruit a volunteer who will come to the class on certain days to provide onetoone help for the child. You can also ask the volunteer to work with the rest of the class so that you can work with the child. Find time to work with the child on a onetoone basis even if only for short periods; for example, when the other children are occupied with other tasks. During this time, try to reduce the distractions such as noise and remove objects not needed for the lesson.

*Teaching strategies*

— Show the child what you want him or her to do rather than simply telling.

— Use simple words when giving instructions and check that the child has understood.

— Use real objects that the child can feel and handle rather than doing paper and pencil work. Try to link the lessons to the child's experiences and everyday life.

— Do one activity at a time and complete it. Make clear when one is finished and a new one is starting.

— Break the task down into small steps or learning objectives. Have the child start with what he or she can do before moving on to harder step. Go back to an easier step if the child encounters problems. For example, in learning to draw a circle; the child can colour in the shape; then move to joining up dots to make a shape; then copy shapes from sample and so on.

— Give plenty of praise and encouragement when the child is successful.

— Give the children extra practice at doing the task – this is sometimes called 'overlearning' but it ensures the child has mastered the skill and increases their confidence. However, be reasonable. Many people with intellectual disabilities remember their school days of being full of doing 'over and over again the same things and never learning new things'.

— The children need to practice the skill with different materials. For instance reading words when they are written on flash cards, on worksheets and reading books. Writing can be practised on the sand, with finger paint, with crayons and pencil and pen. This is called generalising the child's learning.

— Enlist the help of family member who will do 'homework' with the child; revising what has been done in class that day

— Pair the child with peer who can help to focus the child's attention and assist with activities given to the class. Pair the child with more able pupils. When they have finished their work, they can assist the slower child with the task. Assign tasks that they can all contribute to their own level, and work out jointly the assigned task. Assign tasks for a whole group in which the other learners are depended on the contribution of the child with intellectual disability. Other pupils can also be asked to assist the child at break times; use of toilets and so on. For individual tasks, have a number of activities that the child enjoys and can manage on his own so that he does not distract the other children.

— Ignore undesirable behaviour if the child is doing it to get your attention. Give praise and attention when the child's behaviour is acceptable.

A range of different professionals may be able to assist teachers if they are available. For example;

— Speech and language therapists can advise on activities that will help children to acquire and develop language, to learn alternative ways of communication and to improve their speech.

— Physical therapists may be able to suggest activities to help motor coordination.

— Occupational therapists are trained to help with functional skills such as eating and dressing. They can also design or recommend special aids to assist the child with physical impairments to sit or to feed themselves.

— Psychologists may be able to assist with teaching programmes and ways of managing children's behaviour.

— Social workers may be able to assist with family counselling and support.

— Specialist teachers can advise on devising graded learning programmes in range of school subjects. Ideally these professionals will come to the school and the child's home so that they work directly with child, teachers and parents.

*Cerebral Palsy*

Cerebral Palsy (CP) literally means paralysis of the brain. Often the parts of the brain which are most affected control movements of the arms, legs or facial muscles, resulting in limbs being either very floppy or, more usually, very tight and tense. Often people with cerebral palsy find it difficult, or re unable, to talk properly due to difficulties in controlling their head movements or facial muscles.

Cerebral palsy is combination of different disabilities. Sometimes when the damage to the brain is more general intellectual abilities may also be impaired but more often children with cerebral palsy tend to be physically rather than intellectually disabled. Some children may also have difficulties with hearing and/or seeing.

Children may have a mild form of cerebral palsy with minimal loss of function in their limbs or speech defect; to very severe forms when the child is multiply disabled. There is rarely a single cause for cerebral palsy. It may result from congential malformations, maternal infections during pregnancy, birth difficulties and childhood infections such as meningitis, excessive jaundice, rubella and head injury.

There is an increased risk of babies having cerebral palsy with adolescent mothers or those with poor health and living in poverty. For children with mild forms of cerebral palsy, very little adaptations may be needed to classroom. However more severely disabled children may require;

— Special seating to keep their head and body straight when sitting.

— Special desks to work at whose height can be adjusted.

— The use of communication boards so that the teacher and peers can understand the child.

— The child may need extra assistance to use the toilet. Sturdy rails around the toilet will help.

While dealing with children with cerebral palsy the following suggestions can be applied:

— If the child's speech is unclear, devise alternative means for communicating, for example through pictures or drawn symbols. These can be placed together on a board and the child points to the picture to convey the message. Computerised versions are also available. When the child touches the picture or symbol, a synthesised voice says the word.

— Encourage the child to join in answering questions but leave extra time for them to respond either through speech or via symbol boards. Encourage the peers to interact with the child as children usually find their ways of communication.

— Writing will be especially difficult for children if they have problems controlling their hands and arms. They may need extra time to do their writing, or they can be provided with written copy of the information or another pupil may write for them. Computer keyboards can also be adapted to make it easier for children with cerebral palsy to produce written words.

Teachers can take to adapt their classrooms and teaching to overcome the child's difficulties in learning. These are examples of adapting the curriculum. But a curriculum is more than this. Other adaptations may be necessary to remove barriers to learning and participation, For example;

— The level of the content in of the school syllabus
— The outcomes expected from learners
— Equipment and teaching aids used
— Methods used to assess learning outcomes
— Involvement and engagement with families and community.

Remember too that the goal of education is broader than acquisition of knowledge and specific competencies in school subjects. It includes;

— Being able to identify and solve problems using creative thinking
— Collecting, organising and evaluating information
— Collaborating with others in a group or team.

## Conditions Inhibiting Children's Learning

In this section we briefly describe certain conditions that can inhibit children's learning. Teachers may hear these terms used by other professionals or they might come across them in books. These conditions affect children differently; some children might have severe difficulties while with others the affect is mild. Some of these conditions directly affect children's learning. Others are health conditions that teachers need to be aware of.

1) *Aphasia (Specific Language Disorder)*: Some children may have specific difficulties with acquiring language due to some form of brain damage. The children can have difficulty expressing themselves – they get words mixed up – or in understanding what is said to them. This disorder is often confused with

hearing impairments or intellectual disability. Teaching and therapies that are aimed at helping, children to acquire the meaning of words and sentence structures. These can help children overcome their difficulties but it will probably not 'cure' them.

2) *Astma*: The word means 'panting' or gasping for breath. During an asthma attack, the air passages in the lungs become narrow and children have difficulty breathing out. The lungs become blown up. The causes are not fully understood but it is thought that it is due to allergy to substances such as certain foods, pollen from plants and house dust. Attacks may also be triggered by emotional events such as too much excitement or stress such as school examinations. When an attack occurs, children can take medicines to relax the muscles in the lungs, usually through an inhaler. However it is important to remain calm and to reassure the child.

3) *Autism*: This is a controversial term introduced some 40 year ago but some would dispute that a person can be reliably diagnosed as 'autistic'. The essential feature of the condition is that the child has difficulty in communicating; withdraws from contact with other people and appears to be living in his own world. Sometimes people with autistic disorders display remarkable skills focused on one specific area and some appear to become 'normal'. However, no universally recognised treatment exists.

4) *Cleft Palate*: Babies may be born with a deformed mouth and upper lip. They will have difficulty eating and later speaking unless a surgical repair is done to the mouth and lips. They may still have difficulty in

speaking clearly but much of the disability results from others' reactions to their facial deformity is an inherited condition in which the body is unable to use sugar and starch as energy. When there is too much or not enough sugar in the blood, children will feel ill and may even lose consciousness. Feelings of tiredness, lack of concentration, excessive sweating, difficulty in reading and speaking are all symptoms. The children may to have regular insulin injections and they need to careful with what they eat and the amount of exercise they take.

5) *Diabetes*: Children who experience particular difficulty with reading and spelling may be labelled as being 'dyslexic'. However, children with dyslexia are of average intelligence and perform well in other aspects of life. Some children may experience emotional difficulties. They may be very depressed or anxious; or they may show odd behaviours such as crying and laughing inappropriately. They may be excessively active with a short attention span or they may be indifferent, apathetic or absent-minded.

6) *Dyslexia*: The emotional upsets may result from a recent traumatic experience, the death of a parent for example, or they could indicate a more deep-seated, mental health problem. Child psychiatrists may be able to help. Treatments include the use of drugs, counselling and therapy. Teachers can reinforce positive behaviour, or support the child to overcome traumatic experiences, for example.

7) *Emotional/Behavioural Difficulties*: People with this condition experience sudden and uncontrollable 'electrical disturbance' in their brain cells. In severe fits' or 'seizures', as they are called, the person may

lose consciousness and make uncontrollable body movements. Drugs are commonly used to lessen the severity and occurrence of the seizures and many people with epilepsy can lead perfectly normal lives.

8) *Epilepsy*: Epilepsy is prevalent among children with intellectual disabilities but this does not mean that a person who has epilepsy has an intellectual disability.

9) *HIV/AIDS*: Women who have the HIV virus have about a 50% chance of giving birth to a baby who will have the virus. A person with the HIV virus may look healthy. The virus can only be passed on to others in very limited ways; through blood or during unprotected sexual intercourse. It is not possible to get the HIV virus from being near or touching those who have the virus. Hugging, kissing, coughing and sneezing will not spread the disease. Nor can it be spread by toilet seats, glasses, towels and swimming pools. Children who develop AIDS often die young because they cannot fight off other serious illnesses. However the virus can remain hidden for a long time and the children can lead a normal life if given the opportunity to do so.

10) *Muscular dystrophy*: This is a genetic disorder that leads to the degeneration of muscles as the child gets older. The child may start having difficulties in running and climbing stairs and by the teenage years may have to use a wheelchair. Breathing problems due to chest infections are also common. There is no known cure.

11) *Spina Bifida*: The child is born with an incomplete development of bones of the spinal column. This may result in a 'sac' of spinal fluid and nerves protruding

out of the lower back. Surgical intervention is needed to cover the defect as early as possible to prevent infections. The child usually has muscle weakness and the loss of feeling in the lower limbs. A frequent problem is poor bowel and urine control. Hydrocephalus comes from spina bifida. Spinal fluid collects around the child's brain and gives the child a big head. A valve can be inserted into the child's neck to help drain away the fluid. However if this is not done early brain damage can result in intellectual disabilities and visual impairments.

12) *Stammering (or stuttering as it is sometimes known)* is present to some degree in all children as they learn to speak; they stumble over words or repeat the same sounds as they try to pronounce certain words. However it can become a significant problem for some children when they are older. Leave the children time to finish the words or sentences; give praise for their attempts and avoid putting them under pressure to speak.

### *Dealing with diversity in the classroom*

Generally teachers are using nine major ways for dealing with diversity in the classroom.

1. Include all pupils
2. Communicate
3. Manage the classroom
4. Plan your lessons
5. Plan for individuals
6. Give individual help

7. Use assistive aids
8. Manage behaviour
9. Work together

*Include all pupils*: The value of inclusive education to learners comes from mixing and sharing with other children. Teachers need to encourage this to happen as experience suggests that children with special needs can become isolated within classes and schools.

— Teachers may need to explain to other children the reasons why some children cannot talk, behave differently and so on. Diversity should be recognised and respected. Let the pupils discover for themselves how they work together with their peers. Similar work may need to be done at parent-teacher meetings.

_ The biggest obstacle to inclusion is usually negative attitudes. Children may not be accustomed to other children who look and behave differently. Parents may also be worried bout 'lowering the standards' if children with disabilities and other special needs are included in ordinary classrooms. Teachers are instrumental in developing positive attitudes among pupils, parents and of course other teachers.

— Children who use assistive devices such as hearing aids or depend on special equipment can tell the class about it and demonstrate its use.

— Encourage children to 'befriend' pupils with special needs. It is important for social inclusion that children play and work together. They can also assist them at toilets; moving between classroom and at break times.

  — Within the class, develop opportunities for 'peer tutoring'. More able pupils can assist the less able in classwork. Also make sure that children with special needs can also make their meaningful contribution in school work so that they do not become depended and objects of 'help'.

— Devise learning games than pupils can play together in class. Groups of children can play these to help them master reading and number skills.

— Set the class activities to complete as a group; so that all the children can contribute to its completion and gain credit for achieving it.

— Think of how children with special needs can join in games and sports. For example, blind child can be partnered with sighted child in running competitions. Or create a game in which all children move around blindfolded.

— Promote the talents of all children by encouraging their participation in school activities, such as singing, dancing and drama.

— Involve all children in all school activities; for example in cleaning and cooking chores and as class monitors.

— It's a good sign when you see children playing happily together at break times and if they tell you about visiting each other at home.

*Communication*: Communication is central to teaching. Teachers need to communicate with the children; the children with the teacher and with each other. Put simply, communication involves the sending and receiving of messages. For example, the message could be:

— An instruction Write your name in the book

— A question What month comes after June?

— A comment There's a football match on tonight

— An opinion You did that very well

— As you know, teachers have to do lot of talking. Some of the talking is meant to manage and direct the children's behaviour. Sometimes it is to give them new information or to explain new things to them. Other times it is to test their learning.

Communication is central to teaching. Teachers need to communicate with the children; the children with the teacher and with each other. Communication involves the sending and receiving of messages. For example, the message could be:

— An instruction Write your name in the book

— A question What month comes after June?

— A comment There's a football match on tonight

— An opinion You did that very well

— As you know, teachers have to do lot of talking. Some of the talking is meant to manage and direct the children's behaviour. Sometimes it is to give them new information or to explain new things to them. Other times it is to test their learning.

There are many different ways people use. Indeed rarely do we use only one means. Your answer could mention:

— use of gestures –pointing and miming actions

— facial expression to indicate when you are pleased, cross, puzzled

— eye gaze –to indicate who you want to communicate with; or draw people's attention to objects

— pictures and symbols

— reading and writing

— sign languages –such as those used by deaf people

— singing, acting, dancing and touching

Teachers need to make their communication very clear when teaching. All learners are different, some learn best by seeing, other by hearing or doing. A good communicator always uses various channels or ways to communicate and repeats essential contents by using different learning activities in the classroom and elsewhere. Teachers should;

— Be clearly seen by all the pupils –stand rather than sit at the desk.

— Talk clearly and project your voice but not shouting.

— Keep the words simple and the sentences short.

— Alert the pupils to important messages; "listen carefully "–and make eye contact with them if it is culturally appropriate.

— Repeat important messages.

— Use gestures and facial expressions alongside language to get your meaning across. These are especially useful when organising or managing the class.

— Check with the pupils that they have understood. Ask them to repeat what you have said or to say in their own words what you have told them.

— Encourage the children to indicate if they have not understood by raising their hands and asking you questions. They should also do this when they do not understand what other pupils have said.

— Encourage the children to show you and to gesture if you cannot make out what they are trying to say.

— Often classmates or brothers and sisters of a child with a disability are able to tell you what the child is trying to communicate.

— Learn the local sign language and to fingerspell if you have children with hearing impairments. All the class can learn some signs or sign language so that they too can communicate with their peers.

  — Augment your verbal communication with pictures, drawings and writing.

  — Use the 'fourpoint plan' when teaching new skills;

  — Get the child's attention;

  — Present the activity

  — Observe the child's performance

  — Give feedback.

  — Ensure your communications are clear and appropriate for each step.

*Managing Classrooms*: The layout of classrooms can help or hinder children's learning. Perhaps there is not much teachers can do to change their classroom. But here are some ideas.

— Children with special needs need to sit close to the teacher and the chalkboard.

— Try to arrange the room so that children can move freely, especially if some have mobility or visual problems. Likewise, some children might need extra light while some might have light sensitive eyes.

— The children's desks or tables can be arranged in groups so that they can easily work together and help each other.

— If space permits, try to set aside an area of the classroom so that you can work with certain children on a onetoone basis or in small groups for short periods. This area could be screened off using moveable screen to reduce the distractions for the child.

— Have a variety of activities which children can use if they have completed their work ahead of others. This could include a small library of books, worksheets and games.

— Display charts and posters at children's eyelevel rather than high up on the walls. Use large writing, pictures and symbols so that these are easily seen and understood by all children. You can also add different textures and real objects for touching to help children with visual difficulties.

— Some learning is better done outside of classrooms. Using money to buy food can be done in a pretend way in the classroom but even better if children have the opportunity to practice in real settings. Likewise lessons about plants and animals could be done in the school grounds or neighbouring farms.

— Children with visual and hearing impairments may find it more difficult to learn if classes are held outofdoors. Schools may have to arrange for teachers to have suitable rooms if they have such children in their class particularly when they are just starting school.

*Lesson Planning*: When planning a lesson, think of the outcomes you are setting for the class as a whole and then for certain individual pupils. Your Individual Plans will help here. You will then be able to adjust the lesson and the work you want the children to do according to their abilities, interests and motivation. For example, the class may be doing simple addition but one pupil may be given five sums rather than ten to do while another may be working at a simpler level again counting objects into sets. Hence in the one lesson, the teacher works at different levels according to the child's abilities. Think of how you can involve children actively in the lesson. For example, in learning about measurement, the children can find out each other's height!

— Children will be able to understand better if they can see and feel objects. Are there visual aids you can use in your lessons? These can be real objects; pictures or drawings.

— Decide the key words that you will use in the lesson. List these for the children at the beginning of the lesson and try to ensure that they understand them.

— Prepare worksheets to use during the lesson.

These can be designed to meet their particular needs, such as large print if they have visual impairments, or simplified for those with intellectual disabilities. You can keep these for future use. Teachers can swop them with colleagues. However, remember that no two children are alike and you may need to personalise the task. _ Group work facilitates participation of all learners and is an excellent way of responding to individual needs. With special needs pupils, you may need to give them lesson suited to their needs and leave them to do work on this while you teach the rest of the class. However, each lesson should consist of different types of activities; whole class activities, group work, pair work, individual tasks. Use different grouping (mixed /ability /interest groups) and change groups frequently to avoid labelling and 'streaming'.

Teachers may need to adjust the pace of the lesson and the amount of material they cover in the time available. It is better to be selective rather than trying to cover too much material. As well as individual lesson plans, they also need plan for the school day. This will note the alternative activities for children with special needs. It can be helpful to share this plan with pupils at the beginning of lessons.

*Individual Plans*: Teachers need to bear in the mind individual children's needs when planning their lessons. One way of doing this is by having an Individual Plan for each pupil with special needs. This is seen as good practice in many countries and is required by law in some countries. However, it should be reminded that the basis for the lesson planning is the plan for the whole class, and the individual plan can complement the lesson plan to ensure that the learning outcomes are achieved. Individual plans can be made for a full school year, for a term, for individual lessons, etc.

For the primary school child; the plan identifies the specific teaching goals in the main curriculum areas, such as reading and number work. For secondary school pupils, their plan will cover the different subject areas.

— The plan should be drawn up in consultation with the child's parents or careers. In this way, they can identify aspects of the curriculum that they feel is important for their child. It will also help to involve them in assisting the child at home. Parents should be given their own copy of the plan. With older pupils, they can also be involved in the reviewing their plans. They may be able to share with you the difficulties they are finding with their schoolwork.

— The plans are best drawn up at the beginning of each school term. This is a time to review the child's progress in the past term as well as setting new goals. Hence the plans form record of child's progress which can be shared with other teachers as the child moves through the school.

— The plan identifies the child abilities in the different curricular areas. It then notes the new learning goals to be worked on. This means that children in the same class will cover the curriculum to various extents.

— Teachers need to observe or assess the child's level of competence, their interests and specific needs. Identify what they can do by themselves with little or no help from teachers or peers. You can find this out from the work they do in class or you may wish to 'test' their abilities by having them do various graded tasks from easy to hard.

— Deciding on new learning objectives is not easy. These should not be too difficult that the child is discouraged, yet you need to challenge the child to learn new skills. Do not worry about getting it right first time. If the child quickly learns the goals you have selected, you can add others. Likewise if the goals prove too difficult, see if you can break the task down into smaller steps and have the child work on these instead. For example, child may not be able to recognise different coins. Rather than introducing all the coins at once, start with the two that are most different; then introduce another pair; then have pick one from three coins and then from four coins and so on until the child has mastered the task. Teachers often use this step-by-step approach but perhaps with not with such small steps as described in this example.

— The plan should also identify any special arrangements that have proved useful in helping the child at school, such as seating position, use of aids and so on.

*Individual Help*: Children with special needs need support. They therefore benefit more if the teaching is directed to their particular needs. But how can children get individual support? It is not easy but here are some ideas which teachers have found worked them.

When the class are working on an activity, the teacher may spend time with one or two children going over the main points of the lesson with them or helping them to get started on individual work related to the topic of the lesson.

The children can be grouped by ability levels. The teacher can move from one to another to provide assistance tailored to their needs. This works well with reading and number work. However, this should be used in moderation as often ability grouping tends create 'labels' and children quickly identify themselves as belonging to 'winners' or 'losers'. Likewise in mixed ability groupings, the tasks should be designed in such a way that all children can contribute to the task.

Children with special needs can be paired with a more able student who can help them organise their work and assist them when they have completed their own work. This can benefit both pupils. This is known as 'peertutoring'. Two teachers can combine classes. One manages the whole group; while the other spends time doing individual or small group work with the children who need support. Volunteer helpers can be recruited to come into class to assist children. Family members, mothers or grandparents may be able and willing to do this. It may be for a limited period of time to help children settle into classes or to master the basics of certain subjects. Volunteers can support also other children while the class teacher is working with the child with special needs.

Older students in the school can be timetabled to assist students with special needs. This can form part of their social service courses. Volunteers or staff working in Community Based Rehabilitation schemes are another source of individual support. They can be helpful when the child first starts at school, as they will know the child and the family. If your school has access to resource teachers or specialist teachers, they can be called on to support the teachers in planning lessons and appropriate teaching approaches. They could at times give individual support in the classroom. In more affluent countries, teacher's assistants are employed by the school to work in the classroom. Good communication and preplanning between teachers and assistants is essential. Equally the presence of the assistant can inhibit the child with special needs from being an active participant in the class unless the lessons are planned in such a way that all children can be part of the group.

*Assistive Aids*: Children's difficulties can sometimes be overcome by using special and equipment to overcome their particular impairments. Obvious examples are glasses to help children see better; crutches wheelchairs to help them move around school more easily and hearing aids. With younger children, teachers should ensure they wear their glasses and hearing aids in school. Also they need to take care of them as they can be easily broken.

There are other forms of aids which teachers will find helpful. They can be grouped these into five sections. In more developed countries, these can be bought ready-made from suppliers. However it possible to make these at lowcost. Details for making these can be found in the books listed. Older pupils in the school might make these aids as part of their class work. Families can also be asked to help with making them. Children should have the aids at home as well as in school. Schools could build up a 'library' of assistive aids so that teach can share the aids as they need them.

— *Teaching aids*: Teachers often use such aids in their lessons. These can include flashcards to help with reading; wall charts and pictures. The time spent in making aids is worth it as they are a big help to children's learning. Moreover the aids can often be used with other children and shared with other teachers. They need not cost a lot of money as they can be made from scrap materials. Every teacher has the skills to make good teaching aids but they may lack confidence.

— *Practice helps.* Pupils can assist in making the aids. With children who have learning difficulties, you may need to use bigger print or have tactile clues to assist them.

— *Playthings:* A range of playthings for younger children can be made from scrap materials. These include rattles, dolls, puppets, puzzles and musical instruments. Also games such as dominoes can be made larger with raised spots to help children with visual impairments or intellectual disability.

— *Classroom equipment:* Teachers can make equipment to support children's learning. For example, placing foam rubber around pencils so that they are easier for children to grasp; making an abacus from bottle tops to help children count or making rulers with raised or larger numbers for use by children who have visual impairments.

— *Classroom furniture:* Children with physical impairments can have difficulty sitting. They can benefit from special chairs or standing frames that support them correctly. These can be made at little cost from papier-mache or scrap wood. _ Mobility Aids; Various aids can be made at lowcost to help children become mobile. These include trolleys, walking frames and crutches for children with difficulties in walking and the provision of canes for blind children.

— *Communication Aids;* Children can be given a board on which pictures, symbols or words are placed. Teachers and children can then communicate with each other using the board.

— *Managing Behaviour:* Some pupils can be disruptive in class. But children need to learn to behave in a socially acceptable way.

- — All the teachers (and others) involved with the pupil at school should agree on a common approach to responding to the child's behaviour, especially in the use of rewards and punishments.
- — Can you identify cause for the children's behaviour? Are they trying to avoid doing work they find difficult? Do they like getting attention from the other children and the teachers? Are they restless because of hunger? Observing and recording when the behaviour occurs may give some clues as to its cause and the action that is most appropriate for you to take.
- — Pupils will often show warning signs of disruptive behaviour starting. If you can identify these, try to divert the child; for example move closer and put your hand on his shoulder as you continue with the lesson. Or have the child do an activity you know he is capable of and enjoys doing; for example, giving out books to the class.
- — The child may benefit from shorter school day or having times to herself when she can rest. It is better the pupil behaves appropriately all of the time she is in class than be in class behaving inappropriately.
- — The length of time the child stays in class can be gradually increased. This strategy may be useful when first introducing children with special needs to new classes.

— Children who are inclined to run around, could be seated next to the wall or between two other pupils so that they cannot get out so easily. A better strategy is to give active children meaningful tasks to do, such as giving out worksheets and tidying the room so that the tendency of running around can be directed towards an appropriate behaviour.

— Teachers should reward the child when he or she is behaving appropriately and has successfully completed the work set.

— Do this through praise and class recognition. Any plan for dealing with inappropriate behaviours must include the encouragement of positive behaviours. Otherwise the children learn what they are not to do, but they have not learnt what they should do.

— Rewards often work best when the whole class earns a 'treat' for good behaviour. This puts 'peer pressure' on disruptive pupils to behave appropriately. Use tone of voice, facial expression and short, simple sentences to convey your displeasure at pupil's behaviour. Remain calm and in control.

— Punishments are only effective if children can understand the link between it and their behaviour and if it is something they do not like. Likewise do not use extra schoolwork as a punishment.

— Do not threaten the child unless you can carry out the threat and are prepared to do it. Make clear to the child, the consequences of his behaviours. For example, if he hits another pupil, then will he stay in class at lunchtime and not play outside.

— Beware of handing over your authority to others. For example, sending a disruptive pupil to the head teacher gives the message that you are not as important as the head. Both you and the head should see the pupil together.

— Discuss with the students the effects that behaviours can have on one another. The use of drama and roleplay can let pupils experience and release their emotions.

— Find out from the family if the child shows the same behaviours at home. If so, plan with the carers a common approach to reacting to these behaviours.

— Remember; a method, which works with one pupil's behaviour, may not work with another. Planned and consistent responses are the keys to success.

— With particularly severe behaviours the child may need to be withdrawn from the class to work with another adult. However this strategy must form part of a plan in which the suggestions made above feature. Otherwise the pupil may use the behaviour to opt out of class work. Exclusion from the class should be the last resort.

— Secondary schools especially need to work out a policy on suspending and expelling children from schools because of their behaviour. This means that all teachers are following the same procedures and children are being treated fairly. The policy should describe the unacceptable behaviours; the actions that will be taken by class teachers and the school; the contact with families and the length of time the child can be suspended.

— Some children's behaviour is due to emotional problems or reactions to bad experiences. They may benefit for seeing specialist who might be able to identify and help resolve the causes for the behaviour.

*Working Together*: Teachers should not be expected to work only on their own. Here are some ways in which teachers have received advice and support.

— Ask other teachers in your school for advice. This may not common practice nor is it a sign of failure! You can learn great deal from one another. A group of staff could meet once a week for 30 minutes. Each week, teacher takes it in turn to briefly summarise a specific problem; this could be about finding an appropriate method to a teaching task; managing behaviour, etc. The other teachers brainstorm possible ways of dealing with this. The teacher should then select the ones, which seem to offer most promise. Head teachers have an important role to play in developing initiatives such as these.

— Take time to observe how other teachers manage their classes and invite colleagues to watch your teaching. Together you can discuss what you felt went well and areas for improvement.

— The school could send teachers on available training courses. Afterwards they could make a presentation to the staff and share any resources they obtained.

— Find out if there are any disability specialists available in the locality, for example staff in a community based rehabilitation project, or in special schools. Try to meet them to obtain their advice. It is good if they can visit you at school to see the child there and your teaching.

— In some countries, the education authorities have provided 'resource' teachers to assist pupils with special needs. They may be based in one school or they cover a cluster of schools. They can work with classroom teachers in curriculum adaptations and teaching methods. They may also work individually with some pupils or groups of pupils. Teachers should try to observe these sessions and work together with the resource teachers in planning how to incorporate these lessons into their classrooms.

— There are a growing number of books and magazines about supporting learners with special needs. Schools might establish a small library for teachers to consult.

As you have seen there are many ways in which teachers can their practice to better meet the needs of children who are experiencing challenges in learning. But we want to end by stressing things. With some children you will need to make only a few adaptations; others may need more. Even children with apparently the same difficulty will probably require different degrees assistance. Know the child and respond accordingly. Beware of doing too much for the child. The child has to effort into learning as well as the teacher. Gradually do less expect more from the child. Do not ignore the other children in the class as you attend the child with special needs. Try to ensure that the activities planned include all children. Take time at the end of each week to review what's happened.

## Training for Examinations

Examinations are a test of pupil's learning. But taking examinations means much more for the pupil. They have to be able to prepare themselves; to read the examination paper; to express themselves in writing and to be able to write quickly. Children with disabilities may fail examinations because they cannot do these things rather than because they do not know the subject they are being tested in. Equally, some children may be poorly prepared for the examination because of the family situation and low expectations. Thus to be fair to pupils, special arrangements may be needed when it comes to examinations. Here re examples that are in use around the world.

— The pupils are given more time to write their papers. For example, an extra 60 minutes if it is a two-hour examination.

— The pupils have the papers read to them and they can dictate their answer to a teacher who writes it down for marking by another teacher. Pupils can also dictate their answers on cassette. This can assist children with severe visual problems and those with physical impairments that affect their hand movements.

— The students take examinations in fewer subjects.

— The students take only one paper per day. The examinations are more spaced.

— Part of the examination includes a practical test so that pupils can demonstrate their competence without having to use language. This is a better test of pupil's competence if they have language problems.

There other ways in which pupil's competence can be tested other than by writing examination papers or being examined at a specific time and in a special location.

The most common alternative is through continuous assessment. The pupil's learning is assessed over the school year. This can take various forms. For example;

— *Portfolio of work*: The pupil keeps folder of the 'best' work completed during the school year, for example worksheets and completed assignments. This is similar to all the assignments we have asked you to do during this module.

— *Project Work Pupils:* rerequired to undertake a number of projects to test their learning. This may involve independent reading, undertaking 'research' as well as writing report. This is equivalent to the essays and reports that trainee teachers are required to write. Direct observation Teachers can observe a pupil performing various tasks and grade their work on prepared scales. These ratings can be crosschecked by other teachers. This method is particularly useful for practical subjects. Tutors from teacher training colleges use this method when they visit trainee on teaching practice.

— *Functional assessment:* This assessment is in the form of list of competencies that the learner should be able to demonstrate. It is particularly suitable for practical and vocational subjects, such as sewing and carpentry. The pupil has to demonstrate that they can competently undertake the skills outlined in the assessment tool. When you take a driving test, the examiner uses this approach. Students' self-assessment. This is a form of assessment whereby students evaluate their own learning and progress through different means. It gives feedback to both students and teachers. It might require some practice for the students before they can evaluate their performance in an appropriate manner.

All these approaches are better suited to pupils with special needs as they let the students access the extra help and time they may require. Indeed, some would argue that these forms of assessment are fairer to all pupils. But these changes will not come quickly. A starting point is for teachers to adapt the school tests they set for pupils. Here they can experiment with new approaches and refine them so that the methods are fair to all pupils as well as being valid test of the pupil's learning.

Teachers may have little control over the examinations set by the government. However these issues need to be debated nationally and teachers have a vital role to play in this. Change will not happen unless the need for it is made clear. In South Africa for example, their education system is moving away from reliance on examinations to including continuous assessments. But even with existing examination systems, it is worth remembering that many people with disabilities have completed university courses and become successful leaders in industry, education and politics. You could invite them to talk to your students and colleagues.

*Working together*: The challenge of creating education for all cannot be done by one school in isolation. Rather it requires the active cooperation and participation of all the schools within a district –preschool, primary and secondary. This is essential to ensure continuity in the education of children with special needs. Much good work will be undone if a pupil has to transfer schools and the receiving school is not prepared to adapt to his needs. Cooperation among schools is even more crucial if special schools are located in the district. When ordinary and special schools work together, the pupils and teachers in both types of schools will gain.

However, the tradition in many countries is that each school is expected to be self-sufficient with little contact and communication occurring between teachers and pupils beyond competitive games. The educational authorities of course should give a lead in bringing school together. But if this is not forthcoming, then teachers and more especially headteachers can get things moving. Here are some ideas that are emerging from round the world to foster partnerships between schools in supporting each other's efforts towards inclusive education.

— The headteachers of the schools and representatives of the school board of management meet at least once a year to review issues of common concern. This could include reviewing if all the children in the district are enrolled in schools; the admission of children with special needs; access to buildings and equipment; training of staff and support for teachers and children.

— Likewise, teachers can visit each other's schools to learn about the initiatives they have taken in their classrooms to include all children.

— The schools might try to establish in their district a shared resource centre of teaching aids and equipment; books, magazines and video programmes that teachers and families can use. It would ideal if this was linked to a local teacher education institute.

— Teachers may be seconded to another school for period of time. For example, teacher from special school may go to a neighbouring primary school to assist the staff there. This could happen for a period of time –for two weeks – or one day a week for a term.

— In some countries, the education authorities have provided resource teachers to assist pupils with special needs. They may cover number of schools. These resource teachers could convene teachers' meetings; arrange for teacher exchanges and organise training inputs for groups of staff drawn from all the schools for which they have responsibility.

— A group of teachers drawn from all the local schools can be convened to work on topics of mutual interest and need in developing more inclusive schools; such as curriculum adaptations, teaching methods and assessing children's learning. These working groups should have a specific focus and be timelimited. The product can be shared with all schools. This means that work gets done which one school could not do on its own but it also produces shared policies and procedures across the schools.

— If teachers from one school attend training course, on their return they could become a resource for the teachers in other schools in the district; for example by speaking at staff meetings or at parent meetings, or they might organise training inputs for local teachers.

— Groups of schools within an area might invite local 'experts' to present training workshops for all their staff. They may be found in teacher training colleges, universities, Ministry of Education or nongovernmental organisations (NGOs). By combining with other schools, such events will attract reasonable numbers of participants and once again, networks are built among teachers.

— Pupil exchanges can also be encouraged between those in special and ordinary schools. This can take many forms; visiting for social events such as concerts and sharing lessons in particular subjects. Schools that are physically close could base a class in each other's premises to increase the informal contacts pupils have with one another. Also some children in special schools may attend the ordinary school for some or nearly all of their lessons. These sorts of arrangements can be reviewed as the children's needs change. The child may come to spend more or less time in one or other setting.

## Culture Development Strategies

Teachers can help pupils with special needs in many ways at school. But they cannot do everything on their own. They need to work alongside parents, health personnel, community workers and disabled persons' organisations. This may mean changing the cultures of schools. In many countries, schools do not have close links with these groups. But this attitude is changing.

— Children's lives cannot be easily divided into 'school life', 'home life' and 'community life'. Problems in one aspect of their life, will affect the others.

— School is a phase in a child's life. Links need to be made between schools and services for children and families in the preschool years. Likewise schools need to help prepare pupils for life after school.

— The skills needed to live successfully in the society cannot be taught only within school buildings. They need to be carried over into the community.

— Education is everyone's responsibility and should not be left to teachers alone.

The culture and traditions of a school are not quickly changed. One person cannot do it alone. The people with influence must back the change. Such people are;

— The headteacher

— The school board of management

— The school inspectors

— The senior teachers in the school

— Politicians at local and central level

But these important people cannot change things on their own. The teachers, parents and even the pupils have to be willing to make it happen. These groups need to communicate with one another to bring about change. This means;

— Teachers need to meet to discuss their vision for the school and its place in the community.

— The school board of management meets the teachers.

— Meetings are held with parents.

— Discussions take place with educational officials such as inspectors.

The outcome can be an agreed policy on the school's links with the wider community. This helps people outside the school to understand the changes that are taking place. It also gives individual teachers permission to work with other people outside of the school.

*Buiding of Community groups*

— Children with physical and visual impairments as well as those with intellectual disabilities may not be able to walk to school alone. Arrangements need to be made to ensure they get to school safely. Equally some children may have to walk long distances and arrive at school tired.

— Children's health and physical wellbeing must also involve other people.

— What happens when children leave school? Teachers are no longer responsible for them but they need to 'handover' to other people who can take on this responsibility. In addition, other people can assist children with their school work and help teachers in their job. Hence there are very good reasons why teachers need to work in partnership with others.

*Parents role in child education*

Children do best at school when families take a close interest in their education. Some parents or carers may be reluctant to contact the teachers in case they are thought to be interfering. Or perhaps they have had bad experiences at school. Equally parents and grandparents are likely to be the people who know the child best. They are a good source of advice for teachers and the child's main supporters. Schools need to welcome parents. Here re ideas that schools around the world are using. Some parents are more willing than others to become involved. Start with the willing parents and use them to encourage others to join in.

— Parents are invited to meet the child's teacher at least once year to discuss progress.

— Parents are involved in drawing up the individual education plan for the child with special needs.

— Reports on the children's progress are sent to the parents every term.

— Teachers are willing to visit the family at home. This lets them see how the child gets on there.

— Parents are invited to visit their child's class. They can see the teaching methods used in the class.

— Parents can enrich the cultural and ethnic diversity within schools by consulting with them on school practices and involving them in special events and festivals that celebrate their culture.

— Parents are encouraged to assist children with their homework. They could be asked to sign the child's work.

— A notebook goes between home and school with the child each day or at least every week. Teachers and parents can exchange information about the child's school work and learning.

— Parents are asked to help with activities outside school hours, such as sports, choir and school outings.

— Short training courses can be organised for parents. These should focus on practical activities that parents could use at home to help the child learn new skills. Teachers can arrange for visiting speakers to come to these courses.

— Parents can be invited to join some of the training courses that are organised for teachers.

— Parents can be put in touch with the national associations for parents of disabled children. Often they have booklets they can send parents. They may have local branches that parents can join.

— Parents who have children with disabilities are assisted to form local association. Parents can learn from one another. Visiting speakers can talk to the group and answer their questions. The group can press politicians for further help.

— Representatives from the parent groups can be invited to join the board of management for the school.

*Role of health personnel*

Children could have health conditions that hold them back at school. Schools need to foster close links with health personnel. Every country has a network of community health workers. In your community there may also be doctors and nurses you can contact or a mobile health clinic. There could also be specialists such as therapists. Perhaps a community based rehabilitation project is working in your district. This involves trained personnel –either volunteers or paid workers –visiting families at home who have a child or adult with disabilities. They provide suitable aids, give advice on activities to promote selfreliance and income generation, and find ways of mobilising the family and the local community to assist the person.

Schools should keep a list of health personnel and where they can be contacted. This list should be given to all teachers. Schools should invite these persons to visit so that they can meet the headteacher and teachers. Schools can offer their premises to these workers for 'clinics'; for example, to carry out health checks on children in the preschool years. In this way, parents and preschool children become familiar with the school. If teachers suspect children of having health problems, they should refer them to these clinics. Health personnel can be invited to speak at parent meetings or on training courses for parents or teachers. Likewise, teachers may get invited to training courses organised for health personnel. Health personnel already involved with the child and family, such as CBR workers, can be invited to the school. They can contribute to Individual Education Plans for the child. Often appropriate personnel are not available. The school board of management should write to the health authorities and local politicians to point this out. Retired health workers may be willing to offer their services to the school on a voluntary basis. They could assist with developmental checks and screening for disabilities.

*Role of community workers*

The government and NGOs employ various community workers with different roles. They may work with and assist families in many ways. They may organise income generating groups for women or unemployed youth. Or they may lead self-help initiatives such as building projects. Voluntary organisations depend on volunteers. They may be involved in similar activities to employed community workers. In addition they may be leaders in youth organisations or in sports clubs. Schools need to link with employed and volunteer community workers. Many of the suggestions made for health workers apply to these groups as well. For example, they could be offered the use of the school buildings and places on suitable training courses.

Some families can be helped with their basic daily needs and possibly supported to start income generating activities. Community groups could make the school buildings and toilets more accessible for people with physical disabilities. They can build ramps and widen doors so that wheelchairs can be used more easily. Volunteers could make play equipment and teaching aids. Youth organisations and sports clubs can be encouraged to enrol children with disabilities for after school activities. Volunteers can be recruited to assist in the classrooms. Invite reporters from the local paper to any events that the school organises with community workers. This can encourage more people to volunteer.

There are disabled persons' organisations, those run mainly by able-bodied persons for disabled people. Often they raise funds, make donations to individuals and provide services for children and adults. The second type of organisation is made up of disabled people. It is people with disabilities who run the association. They aim to promote the rights of disabled people rather than fundraise or provide services. However, many offer training and support for their members. Parents of children with different disabilities have also come together in associations. These associations also provide information and advice to their members through meetings and publications. They may also organise services such as preschools or vocational training.

All these different associations are usually based in capital cities. Some have local branches throughout the country. Often each association concentrates on a specific disability. In some countries a federation of disability organisations has been formed with the aim to press for equal rights, better services and to educate communities about disability. The advantages for greater contact between schools and disabled people's organisations or Parent Associations are these;

— The associations can give teachers advice and guidance on how to deal with specific disabilities.

— They can supply information leafiets for parents.

— They may be able to provide special equipment and devices to assist the pupil in school or at home.

— Members of the association could be available for training teachers and parents. For example, deaf people can teach sign language.

— The members can be valuable rolemodels for young people with disabilities.

— Schoolleavers can be encouraged to join the associations and to go on training courses they organise.

— They may be willing and able to do fundraising for schools either locally or internationally.

— Keep a list of disabled persons' organisations and parent associations both locally and nationally.

— Invite adult persons with disabilities to visit the school to meet with pupils and teachers.

— Encourage the formation of selfhelp group of people with disabilities in the locality.

— The formation of parents associations can also be encouraged to provide mutual support and assist the schools in planning to meet the children's needs.

*Role of community supporters*

Young people with special needs can find it difficult to find their place in society. This can be especially true when school years are over. The common concerns for schoolleavers are;

— No employment

— Few friends and difficulty finding a partner

Teachers need to look outside the school and work in partnerships with others who can support the young people. If schoolleavers can get employment, there is a greater chance of them making friends and getting their own accommodation. Here re some ways teachers are doing this.

*Role of vocational classes*

Many secondary schools have developed more practical curriculum for their students with special needs. This concentrates on lifeskills rather than academics. Students learn to look after their personal needs, such as washing clothes and cooking. They also learn some job skills – sewing, woodwork are common examples. The job skills should be relevant for the needs of the community. Training is also given in managing money and interpersonal skills. Volunteers from the community are recruited to assist with these programmes.

*Importance of work experience*

Find employers who will take the young person into their business so that they can experience the work that is done there. They are not paid but the employer is expected to train them in some jobs that they could learn to do. This gives the young person a chance to prove themselves as well as learning to deal with new situations.

— *Vocational training* : Schoolleavers can be enrolled in courses that train them for work. If these centres have not taken people with disabilities before, they may need some help and support. The schoolleavers might attend on a parttime basis to get familiar with the people and the trainers with them.

— *Family businesses* : Parents can be encouraged to help the young person set up their own business or to assist in the family business. This can start from in the teenage years and could link with the lifeskills curriculum mentioned earlier.

— *Further Education*: A person's chances of getting job re increased if they have further education. Young people with special needs should be encouraged to apply for college or university courses.

— *Employment*: Young people with special needs can apply for jobs in just the same way as other young people. However they all need to learn about the skills needed for jobs and their competence to do a job. They may need training in completing application forms and personal presentation at interviews.

# 5

# Planning and Challenges of Adult and Literacy

The way people think about and plan for development began changing in the 1980s. Until then most development programmes were based on the assumption that societies progress inevitably, but over varying periods of time, to modernity. The goal, therefore, was to help the 'developing' nations to establish the value systems, practices and infrastructures that would accelerate their socio-economic progress and make them like the more 'developed' ones. Newer definitions focus on community-building rather than on modernization.

Development is conceptualized as a process in which individuals, living and working together, grow in their ability to define problems, plan solutions, and initiate and control constructive change. The concern, therefore, is less with increasing industrialization and expanding the economy and more with encouraging and supporting people as they take responsible control of the world around them. As conceptions of development have evolved, so have conceptions of literacy and its role in the development process.

'Traditional' approaches considered literacy a technical skill that involved decoding and encoding written symbols. The assumption was that before people could gain meaning from and use the written word, they had to learn to match correctly the marks on a printed page with their corresponding sounds. Once they had mastered these basic skills, the new literates should continue to gain fluency and the ability and motivation to use reading, writing and numeracy for their own purposes. Newer approaches to literacy consider reading as more than encoding and decoding printed symbols.

Literacy is seen as an integral part of development, a tool that helps learners understand better the political and social forces that impact their lives. This social and political awareness is not a goal that is reached after learners gain basic reading, writing and numeracy skills. Rather, both the content of the lessons and the manner in which literacy and numeracy are taught should enable learners to gain the confidence and ability to participate actively in decision-making on matters that affect them.

Perceptions of policy formulation and implementation began changing in the 1980s. Before that time the general perception was that the two tasks were distinct and sequential activities-that when policy formulation ends, implementation begins. Research beginning in the late 1970s, revealed instead that the two are not distinct processes but compose a cycle that repeats itself throughout the life of a programme: policy is formulated, implemented, assessed, adapted, further implemented, re-assessed, and so on.

This reconceptualization of the process provides several valuable insights for literacy planners. It sees assessment as integral to the decision-making and implementation process. It also emphasizes the importance of collaboration between planners, implementers, and managers at each level of the programme and of built-in flexibility that allows programme plans to be adapted as needed.

In development-oriented approaches to literacy, each group of stakeholders – those who provide financial and other support for the programme, those who take overall responsibility for implementation and management, and the prospective learners themselves – is represented in decision-making. Shared decision-making helps to ensure that programmes are relevant to the people they are meant to serve and encourages a sense of mutual responsibility and ownership – essential ingredients for sustainability.

Several small-scale literacy programmes in West Africa illustrate this participatory approach at the local level. In Cameroon, committees in each community took responsibility for mobilizing support for their adult literacy programme and identifying the community's needs that would be served by it. In Côte d'Ivoire, a bilingual literacy programme began with numeracy rather than reading and writing because that was the need identified by the learners. And in mother-tongue literacy projects in Ghana, people in each community took responsibility for all aspects of their programmes, from selecting teachers to preparing and distributing literature.

The process of participatory decision-making is not without its problems. Stakeholders might agree on their programme's goals, for example, but not on the means for achieving them. Different groups may have different priorities or they may not share the same sense of urgency about different components of their programme. They may disagree about who should be in leadership or how resources should be used. Those with overall responsibility for the programme may conclude that involving people in decision-making takes longer and is less 'efficient' than doing the job themselves. Also, the people who are invited to participate may be confused and intimidated by the system they have been invited to join. The decision for stakeholders is whether the short- and long-term benefits to the programme and to its beneficiaries are worth the difficulties they might encounter.

## Challenges of Adult Literacy Programmes

In programmes that are learner-centred, guiding principles are the product of dialogue among representatives of all the stakeholder groups. A guiding principle for a community-wide adult literacy programme might be: 'Instructional methods and reading materials should affirm and build on the learners' life experiences.' Guiding principles for a nationwide or statewide programme might be: 'Supporting agencies should work together rather than compete with each other to implement and manage the programme.' Another guiding principle might be that, 'At each level and at each place of implementation, priority should be given to identifying and utilizing resources that are already available, rather than depending on outside resources to sustain the programme.'

A programme's goals describe in general terms what the stakeholders hope will happen in the future as a result of the literacy programme – its intended long-term consequences for the learners, the community, the education system, and for the nation as a whole. They describe an ideal future but are realistic so that stakeholders will be encouraged as they see themselves making progress.

Goals for learner-centred literacy programmes are congruent with national policies and plans and also with the educational goals of the prospective learners – their reasons for wanting to be literate. In a city-wide literacy programme for out-of-school or unemployed youth, for example, a goal formulated by the learners might be that they will have the knowledge, skills and motivation to find and keep gainful employment.

An additional goal of the programme – this one formulated by the programme's sponsors –might be that the crime rate among the city's youth will be reduced. A goal for a state-sponsored transitional literacy programme for new immigrants might be that the immigrant-learners will become an integral part of their new society (a goal of the sponsors) and also become fluent in the language of their new country (an additional goal of the learners).

The process of setting goals begins by seeking agreement among stakeholders at each level of implementation about why the programme is needed – the problems it is meant to solve – and achieving a consensus regarding the overall purpose it will serve. At national and sub-national levels, goal-setting might be the focus of early planning sessions involving representatives of the different groups who will implement, manage and support the programme at that level, together with representatives of the prospective learners. At local level, a community's goals for literacy might be formulated through formal meetings and informal discussions with the prospective learners, community leaders, and with local government agencies and NGOs.

Objectives describe the specific targets that are to be reached within the period of time covered in the programme plan. They are the explicit statements on which the programme will be periodically assessed in the process of achieving the programme's long-term goals. Objectives are flexible so that they can be adjusted if assessment reveals that they are unrealistic or that they are not serving the purposes for which they were planned.

An objective for a community literacy programme for out-of-school youth might relate to the number of learners that will complete the course in the first two years. At sub-national level, an objective might state the number of teachers that will be trained within a specific time period or the number of training centres that will be established. A national-level objective might list the number of states or provinces in which literature production centres will be established in the first three years. Whether planning takes place at national, sub-national, or local levels, the process of formulating objectives requires knowledge of the resources and activities that are necessary for the programme to be sustained, as well as awareness of the resources that are already available and the activities that are already taking place.

Decisions about the size and scope of a literacy programme are influenced by the needs and goals of the learners and by the political, economic and sociocultural context in which the programme will take place. Three common approaches are the mass campaign and large-scale and small-scale projects.

Mass campaigns are usually initiated by the government and depend on sustained and intensive government leadership at national, sub-national and local levels, usually with the support of relevant NGOs. The goal of a campaign is to make large numbers of people literate within a specified time-frame in order to consolidate large-scale social and/or political changes. Vast human and material resources are mobilized. Decision-making is centralized, although day-to-day management may be localized. Curricula and instructional materials focus on issues that the government considers important, although there may be flexibility in adapting the ideas to local contexts.

Viet Nam's literacy programme is an example of a mass campaign, actually three separate campaigns, initiated between 1954 and the late 1970s. The purpose of the campaigns was to promote national unity and economic growth through a more literate populace. Teacher-training workshops stressed patriotism as well as instructional strategies. The government provided full-time instructors and learning materials but village co-operatives were expected to take responsibility for funding first- and second-level classes. Decisions made at the national level were carried out by volunteers in local communities. All three campaigns were implemented in the midst of armed conflict and economic embargoes and without outside funding or support.

Nicaragua's literacy crusade was also intended to develop a new and unified national identity. The programme was initiated by the new government in 1980 but planning and decision-making were to be more decentralized. A National Co-ordinating Commission consisting of 25 ministerial, political, military, educational, cultural, religious, and 'mass' or local organizations was established within the Department of Education to set overall policy and facilitate implementation.

Parallel co-ordinating commissions were also established at departmental and municipal or local levels. Most of the actual planning for implementation took place at the municipal level. And it was in the municipalities that organizations worked together most co-operatively and that participation of the intended beneficiaries was greatest.

An advantage of the campaign approach is that government power and resources are put at the disposal of the literacy programme. Governments have the means of establishing a favourable political climate and mobilizing resources and popular support that usually are not available to smaller programmes.

A disadvantage of the campaign approach is that maintaining the programme over a long period of time requires a level of political and economic commitment that few governments are able or willing to sustain. Another potential problem is that a mass campaign, with its top-down approach to decision-making, might discourage the level of 'grass-roots' initiative and ownership that is necessary if the literacy programme is to survive when government support declines. A third potential disadvantage is that a mass campaign can be a tool for political indoctrination rather than for promoting equity. Finally, the mass campaign approach is ill-suited to multilingual and/or multicultural contexts. Centralized curricula and materials are ineffective if learners do not understand the language of instruction and if the content of the lessons does not relate to their own educational goals.

Large-scale projects also cover multiple political, geographic, and/or sociocultural areas, but they lack the intensity and unifying focus of mass campaigns. Primary responsibility for large-scale projects may rest either with a government agency or with one or more NGOs, or the programme may be under the joint sponsorship of a government agency and an NGO working in co-operation.

Overall goals and objectives may be established by the sponsoring agencies but because there is less control from the 'top', decisions are more easily adapted to sub-national and local contexts. Decisions about the language of instruction and content of the lessons, for example, may be left to local communities.

An example of a large-scale project is the national Literacy and Awareness Programme in Papua New Guinea, established by the government in 1989 to support NGOs and communities that had been conducting their own small-scale projects for decades. Responsibility for the smaller projects remained mostly with the groups that had originally initiated them.

Government support involved developing curriculum guidelines and prototype reading materials that could be adapted to different language and cultural situations, sponsoring training workshops, and allocating grants to NGOs and communities for teacher training and literature production.

An advantage of large-scale projects that are established in response to grass-roots' initiatives is that they build on infrastructures already in place at sub-national and local levels. The decentralized structure tends to reduce top-down control, leaving decisions about individual programmes to the people who know best what is needed and what will work in their situation. Curricula and reading materials, for example, can be modified to fit the educational goals of the learners.

A possible disadvantage is that a large-scale programme needs the ongoing co-ordination and support of a central agency. If the programme is dependent on the voluntary involvement of NGOs, it may be endangered if the NGOs leave or lose their funding. Decentralized control may also result in duplication of efforts if, for example, each of the supporting NGOs produce their own curriculum frameworks or teaching guides or establish their own materials production centres. Finally, the use of multiple languages can complicate the development of reading and teaching materials and may place a burden on limited human and material resources.

Small-scale projects are geared to a specific audience (a single language group or dialect, a single community, or a single interest group within a community) and serve a specific purpose (health education, family planning, income generation, etc.). They are usually sponsored by an NGO that also takes responsibility for training teachers and providing instructional and reading materials.

The Adivasi adult literacy programme in Andhra Pradesh Province in India is an example of a small-scale project. Integrated with a local development programme, its purpose is to help people become literate in their mother tongue in order to facilitate their transition to Telegu, the regional language, and improve their economic conditions. Local institutions take responsibility for managing and supervising the programme, developing curriculum and reading materials, and recruiting and training personnel.

Small-scale projects usually originate outside the bureaucracy and in close co-operation with the learners. They tend to be more flexible than large-scale projects or campaigns and are able to respond more rapidly to the changing needs of the people they serve. The most obvious disadvantage of small-scale projects is that they reach relatively few people. And because of their narrow support base, small projects are endangered if local infrastructures have not been firmly established and local people have not been equipped to maintain them.

In multilingual contexts, choosing a language for literacy, or for education in general, is a complex task that must take into account a multitude of social, cultural, economic and political factors. Some governments choose to use a single language in their campaigns or large projects in order to promote national unity or to ease the burden of producing literacy materials and training teachers. Others contend that using a single language serves a 'gate keeping' function: only minority language speakers who are willing to sacrifice their traditional languages and cultures are able to move successfully through the education system. Some who advocate mother tongue for early education also contend that too great a cognitive burden is placed on learners who "are expected to learn in a foreign language from teachers who are speaking a foreign language, using materials written in a foreign language, about concepts that are foreign to everyone's personal experience". Until the 1980s, large-scale mother-tongue literacy programmes in multilingual societies, with or without later transfer to a dominant language, were rare.

Relatively few governments had developed language and literacy policies that supported multilingualism and fewer still had made the commitment in time and resources that were required to develop and maintain literacy programmes in multiple languages. Among the exceptions were pre-primary education programmes in Namibia and Papua New Guinea.

The intent of the programmes in these two countries was to teach children in their local language for the first three years of school, after which they moved into primary grades in which English was the language of instruction. These nationwide programmes for children could serve as models for large-scale adult literacy programmes elsewhere if sponsoring agencies are prepared to make the commitment that is required for such efforts.

Another issue for planners to consider relates to the type of classes that will be established to serve the specific needs of the learners and build on the abilities they already possess. Four general types of classes can be identified, based on four general stages of literacy.

Basic literacy classes are for people who have had little or no previous formal or non-formal education but whose personal and occupational goals require literacy and numeracy. Curriculum, instructional methods, and reading materials build on the learners' well-developed understanding of their language and culture and begin immediately to encourage them to be involved actively in the affairs of the world around them.

In fluency classes, readers who have achieved a basic level of proficiency consolidate and expand their uses of reading, writing and numeracy to meet their expanding educational goals. Fluency classes might also be established to help more literate adults move into the formal education system or into vocational training programmes by preparing them for entrance examinations or introducing them to the kinds of reading materials they will be expected to use in the ongoing education programme.

In bilingual or multilingual contexts, transitional classes are for people who have become proficient readers in their mother tongue and now want to transfer their literacy skills into a second (or third) language. Labelling this type of literacy class 'transitional' assumes that the learners already speak the second language and are now ready to learn to read and write in it.

Post-literacy educational opportunities enable learners to continue their education in the formal or vocational systems or through special interest classes, reading clubs, and other educational opportunities in their local communities. Equally important to adults who have reached the post-literacy stage is the variety of reading materials that are interesting and relevant to them.

Decisions about the type of classes that will be established are best when they are based on prospective learners' own assessments of their ability to use literacy to achieve their goals. For example, out-of-school youth who had attained a basic reading ability in primary school may have relapsed into semi-literacy once they left the formal system.

Fluency classes could help them to regain and expand on what they had learned previously in order to prepare them for further education or help them learn specific skills for employment. In multilingual situations, transition classes might be appropriate if community members who are already literate in their mother tongue, want to become literate also in their second language.

The Adivasi people of India learned to read and write in their mother tongue in order to ease their transition to literacy in Telegu, the regional language. In other cases, people who are already literate in their second language want to transfer back to their mother tongue.

The Government of Paraguay, for example, initiated special literacy classes in the formal education system for Guarani-speaking students who had been required to learn to read and write in Spanish, the language of education, but still were most comfortable using Guarani, their mother tongue .

At the local level, educational differences among the learners also influence the way classes are organized. A women's group, for example, might choose to divide itself into two separate classes if some members have achieved a measure of fluency while others are still at the basic literacy stage. On the other hand, the two groups might choose to stay together so that the more advanced readers can tutor the beginners. Decisions about the way to divide and/or organize their classes, then, would be based on the abilities, attitudes and goals of the women themselves.

The guiding principles, goals and objectives, established through dialogue among all the stakeholders, will, hopefully, influence decision-making throughout the life of the programme. Decisions relating to the size and scope of the literacy programme, the language(s) that will be used, and the type(s) of literacy classes that will be established will affect later decisions about other components of the programme such as teacher training and materials production. These preliminary decisions, and the manner in which they are made, will also affect the way the programme is perceived by the multiple stakeholders and, therefore, the degree to which it is accepted by them.

## Strategies for Programme Implementation

Most strategies for literacy include six component plans:

— *Preliminary research*: collecting information that will be used to plan the programme.

— *Promotion*: generating and nurturing interest and a sense of ownership for the programme among the intended beneficiaries and supporters.

— *Recruitment and training*: identifying the personnel that will be needed for the literacy effort, developing criteria for recruitment, and planning pre-service and in-service training.

— *Curriculum development*: defining educational goals and intended learning outcomes, developing curricula and teachers' guides, and, at community level, planning the content of the lessons.

— *Materials development and production*: identifying topics that are of interest to the learners; developing infrastructures or support systems for writing and illustrating reading materials and for producing and distributing them to local communities.

— *Evaluation*: determining if the literacy programme is achieving its objectives, if it actually is serving the needs of the intended beneficiaries, and, therefore, if it is in the process of achieving its long-term goals.

These six strategic elements are common to most literacy programmes, regardless of their size or location. Whether for a state-run transitional literacy programme for immigrants in London, a community-based literacy programme sponsored by a local women's group in Kenya, or a mass literacy campaign in Nicaragua, a literacy programme strategy would include, for example, a plan for promotion or mobilization – for informing the public of the programme and encouraging their participation in it. These same six strategic elements are also common across levels of implementation and administration.

Using promotion again as an example, a large-scale literacy programme needs to be promoted among government departments, funding agencies and supporting NGOs at sub-national, national and international levels, as well as among potential learners and supporters at the local level. But while the six general strategic elements are common to most successful literacy programmes, the manner in which they are implemented is specific to each context. An 'action plan' for each element might include the following components:

1) identifying the activities that will be carried out to implement the plan in that context;

2) establishing the time-frame for completing each activity;

3) identifying the people who will be responsible for each activity and the resources that will be needed; and

4) identifying the factors that might hinder successful completion of the activity and the possible means for overcoming these problems.

Let us describe the basic strategic elements necessary for implementing sustainable literacy programmes. Each element is examined in relation to its purposes and to the issues and questions that should be considered in planning for its implementation and maintenance.

### *Research needs*

Preliminary research involves identifying, collecting and interpreting the information that will be needed to make planning decisions. Preliminary research requires two kinds of expertise: the technical expertise of the education specialists and the sociocultural expertise of the people who will be responsible for the local programmes. The research team might use one or more methods for gathering information, depending on the research objectives, the time and resources available, and on the type of relationship that planners want to begin developing with the different stakeholders:

— *Informal discussions*: Informal discussions with the intended beneficiaries of the programme can be the means for identifying the learners' needs and goals on which curriculum and reading materials will be based. Before beginning a basic education programme among poor people in rural Colombia, staff from the Ministry of Education met with community members to identify their immediate and long-term education goals and to determine what educational activities would best respond to their concerns and expectations. This information formed the basis for the plan for that area.

— *Formal meetings*. Formal meetings with relevant government and non-government agencies can be used to promote the programme as well as to gather information for planning. In Papua New Guinea, the local co-ordinator of a mother-tongue literacy programme met with district and provincial education officers to inform them of the programme, learn from them what government resources might be available for it, and encourage them to participate in planning and decision-making.

— *Survey instruments.* Different survey instruments can be prepared for different populations. Questionnaires can be mailed to literate individuals and interview forms can be used in individual and group interviews. Their purpose might be to collect information for a literacy database and to learn about people's attitudes and perceptions with regard to the literacy programme Group interviews have an added benefit in that responses can be used to stimulate further discussion and problem-solving by the respondents.

— *Mass media.* Electronic and print media can be used for research and for promoting the literacy programme. For example, radio broadcasts or newspaper articles dramatizing or discussing the potential benefits of literacy can conclude with an invitation to listeners or readers to send information to programme sponsors about literacy needs in their community and about literacy programmes that have already been established in their areas.

### *Promotion of literacy development programmes*

Literacy-for-development programmes are people-centred: they consider intended beneficiaries as partners in rather than targets of development and are a product of ongoing collaboration among the different groups of stakeholder. The purpose of promotion, then, is first to encourage the non-literate public to think critically about the specific ways that literacy might benefit them and the problems it might help them solve, and secondly to encourage people's active participation in planning and maintaining the programme. This approach to development may be especially important in situations in which intended beneficiaries have been left out of decision-making in the past. Promotion serves specifically to:

— Provide preliminary information about the literacy programme and about what will be necessary to establish and maintain it.

— Invite representatives of each of the stakeholder groups –donors, government officials, NGOs, and prospective learners – to work together in planning the programme for their respective areas and begin identifying and/or developing the infrastructures that will be necessary to sustain it.

— Encourage stakeholders to begin identifying resources that can be used for implementation and maintenance and inform them of any additional outside assistance that will be available.

The possibilities for promotion are limited only by the ingenuity of the planners in making use of available resources. At local level, for example, skits can be performed at public gatherings. Schools can hold contests in which students draw pictures illustrating the value of literacy and winning entries can be posted around the community. Literate people in the community can write to government agencies, NGOs, businesses, and other potential supporters and donors to invite their involvement. At sub-national and national levels, radio stations can broadcast programmes about literacy, provide air time for listeners to call in with questions, and make regular announcements about literacy classes that are being planned. Newspapers can publish articles and stories. Formal ceremonies at national, sub-national and local levels can be held to inaugurate the literacy effort.

### *Recruiting of literacy personnel*

Recruiting for a literacy programme involves identifying the activities that will take place in implementing and maintaining the programme, determining the qualifications that will be needed by the personnel responsible for these activities, and securing the services of people with those qualifications. Training involves helping these people gain the motivation, knowledge and competencies to function creatively and effectively in their positions.

The process of establishing qualifications and selecting people for the different positions is influenced by the programme's guiding principles, goals and objectives and by the context in which the different activities will take place. At each level of implementation, personnel for learner-centred literacy programmes require special personal attributes in addition to their technical and professional qualifications. They should be resourceful in adapting ideas and information to their specific situations and respected by the people with whom they work. They should appreciate the social, cultural and linguistic backgrounds of the different groups of learners and be committed to helping individuals and communities achieve their educational goals. While specific activities will vary, strategies for recruitment include several components:

— Identifying the activities for which personnel will be required at each level of implementation.

— Determining the criteria for recruiting personnel for each position at each level, based on a realistic assessment of the people that might be available.

— Identifying the financial and/or other support that different personnel will require and projecting the ability to provide that support. The amount of funding available will influence the degree to which the programme must rely on volunteers who may or may not be available.

— Planning the method of recruitment. At national and sub-national levels, procedures for recruitment follow the policies and practices of the respective government departments and NGOs.

Recruiting personnel at local level begins by informing community members of the essential qualifications for people in each position and asking them to identify people that have these qualifications and are acceptable to the community in general.

Training as an ongoing process. Training for learner-centred adult literacy programmes has both a formal component and an informal component. Ideally, formal and informal training share several general characteristics:

— Trainees participate in identifying what they need to learn and in assessing their own learning progress.

— Trainees and trainers have mutually supportive relationships.

— Adult learning characteristics are emphasized, especially as they differ from those of children.

— Trainees are encouraged to adapt what they have learned so that it is appropriate in their local situation.

— Training of trainers is a priority. Experienced teachers who have demonstrated special skills and sensitivity are encouraged and equipped to become trainers.

Formal and informal training for learner-centred literacy builds on the knowledge and experiences of the trainees as well as on the expertise of the trainer and encourages dialogue in which each facilitates the other's learning. A mutually supportive training process provides a model for trainees to follow later in their own classrooms. Helping teacher trainees to see themselves as facilitators and co-learners can be a long and difficult process, especially for those whose previous learning experiences emphasized knowledge as a product transferred from teacher to passive students rather than generated through participatory activities.

Trainees need ongoing opportunities to observe experienced teachers who demonstrate the desired attitudes and behaviour in their classroom and to practice under their tutelage. Ideally, then, the training process for new teachers would involve:

(1) several weeks observing an experienced teacher in a classroom situation;

(2) attending a training workshop;

(3) practice-teaching under the experienced teacher; and

(4) attending in-service training workshops on a regular basis to meet specific training needs as they arise.

*Curriculum and instructional methods*

In programmes that consider learning to be a self-directed, participatory process, curriculum and instructional methods are designed to help learners to achieve their personal goals for literacy. Decisions about curriculum and instruction, therefore, take into account general characteristics of adult learners:

— They possess a great deal of experience and knowledge relating to a variety of topics, are aware of their own problems, and have their own educational goals.

— They do not learn the same way as children do and do not want to be taught the same way as children are taught.

— They have many responsibilities and do not want to be involved in activities that they feel are a waste of time.

— They may be uninterested in individualized learning and uncomfortable in competitive situations or, conversely, they may enjoy competition and learn best on their own.

— They may lack self-esteem because of their inability to use print media, because they have had previous unsuccessful school experiences, because of their low social status or – if they are members of an ethnic minority – because of the low status of their language and culture.

The process of curriculum development, begins by learning about the learners themselves and identifying what they want to learn. During the planning phase, efforts are made to determine the prospective learners' educational goals, the reasons why they want to become literate. Women in a rural village in Asia, for example, might want to read, write and calculate so that they can start and maintain an income-generating project. These women's educational goals would be to be able to keep business records and to maintain their own bank accounts.

Although there are many differing definitions of curriculum, the term here refers to the organized collection of intended learning outcomes – the knowledge, skills, attitudes, and behaviours that will enable adult 'learners' to achieve their educational goals . Intended learning outcomes for the rural Asian women would be the specific knowledge and skills relating to reading, writing and numeracy that will be necessary for them to keep business records and maintain bank accounts. Implied in this definition of curriculum is the possibility that the set of intended learning outcomes may be inadequate – that even though the learners gain the knowledge and skills prescribed in the curriculum, they still may be unable to meet their educational goals.

Curriculum development requires ongoing evaluation of learning outcomes to see if the curriculum truly is enabling learners to achieve their educational goals. If the intended learning outcomes are achieved but the educational goals have not been reached, the curriculum needs to be revised. If the educational goals answer the question 'why', and the curriculum answers the question 'what', the instructional method answers the question 'how'. The instructional method includes all the planned learning activities that are used to achieve the intended learning outcomes.

The approach that literacy providers take to curriculum and instruction is influenced by their own perceptions of 'literacy'. On the one hand are those who consider literacy to be a technology that literate people use for their own purposes. Based on that point of view, becoming literate is an educational process, but not necessarily a political one.

Curriculum and instructional methods are meant to help adult learners acquire gradually the technical skills and behaviours that the providers consider essential to reading and writing fluency. The assumption is that having gained the essential technical skills, the learners will be able to use the skills for their own specific purposes.

An alternative approach to literacy is based on the assumption that the process by which people learn to read, write and calculate influences the way they will use reading, writing and numeracy in their lives. Those who take this approach argue that curriculum and instructional methods should grow out of the learners' social context and immediately begin encouraging them to think about the ways they can use literacy to solve the problems they have identified and to achieve their personal goals.

Curricula and instructional methods that are meant, for example, to help adult learners improve their income-earning potential would be different from those meant to help them gain access to their religion's sacred writings or to communicate their community's needs more effectively to governmental agencies. Planning for curriculum development. If there are not enough specialists to prepare a curriculum for each group of learners, curriculum frameworks developed at sub-national, national and international levels can be adapted to the educational goals of the different learning groups.

A curriculum framework is a pattern or outline that helps teachers to organize their curriculum under different topics – health, community life, and culture, for example – that are of general relevance to the adult learners in that area. The topics and curriculum content can then be adapted to each group of learners. The process for developing, adapting, using and revising a curriculum framework for adult literacy might include the following steps:

— In national or sub-national workshops, curriculum specialists and experienced teachers develop a curriculum framework for adult literacy classes built around general topics of national or regional interest that can be modified to meet the educational goals of the individual groups of learners.

— In dialogue with the prospective learners, teacher-trainees in local communities identify the learners' educational goals and the specific topics that are interesting to them.

— At pre-service training workshops, teacher-trainees become familiar with the purpose, content and instructional method associated with the curriculum framework and then modify the framework to their learner-identified topics.

— Trainees practise teaching the lessons they have prepared to other participants. This practice teaching helps them to become familiar with the curriculum and enables them to identify and correct problems with their instructional methods.

— In the learners' communities, the curriculum is tested in pilot classes and revised as necessary.

*Developing learning materials*

Adults generally do not learn to read because someone tells them they should. They do so because they have certain goals and they believe that literacy will help them achieve those goals. If literacy does indeed serve their purposes, they will continue to use it as a resource. If it does not, they are likely to lose interest and, eventually, whatever abilities they had gained in reading and writing. Unfortunately, this point is often overlooked by planners at international as well as national, sub-national, and local levels. A common factor in the poor long-term survival rate of literacy programmes is that planners did not foresee the ongoing need for a variety of interesting and relevant reading materials in the languages of the readers. Self-sustaining infrastructures for literature development (writing, illustrating, and editing books, games, posters, etc.) and production (printing or duplicating the materials using offset press, photocopiers, duplicators, or silk-screen printers) are essential for ongoing literacy. Four general types of materials can be identified:

— Materials that introduce the reading process. Reading materials for early literacy classes help new readers to become familiar with print literature and to begin to experience the ways that literacy can help them to achieve their educational goals. Stories about familiar topics and experiences may be limited in length and complexity, but not so much that language becomes stilted and unnatural. Functional materials such as banking deposit and withdrawal slips or business order forms can also be introduced at this stage if the materials are relevant to the learners' educational goals and in a language they understand, and if the learners are already familiar with the contexts in which the materials are used.

— Materials that help learners to gain fluency. The purpose of materials at this stage is to help learners to increase their confidence in using print media and challenge them to expand their uses of reading and writing to meet their daily needs and to be active participants in the development process. New ideas are introduced as materials increase in length and language complexity.

— Materials that help people to transfer reading and writing from their first to their second language. Materials at this stage assume that readers already speak and understand the new language. Dictionaries, phrase books, books of legends, songs, poetry, and stories in their first and second languages are needed for readers at this level.

— Materials for lifelong education. Once they have achieved fluency in their spoken languages, adult learners are able to use the printed word for a multitude of purposes that require access to an increasing variety of literature. Unfortunately, it is at this point that the system often breaks down, especially in minority language groups without a long written tradition. Planning infrastructures for literature production that will continue to provide readers with relevant and challenging reading materials are essential for meeting the needs of this reading audience. A common tendency in materials production for adult literacy programmes, especially those that are centrally initiated and controlled, is to focus on functional topics or on topics that promote civic consciousness and national unity – topics that are considered important to the central planners. But as people living in a community, learners have other reasons for reading in addition to their functional and civic needs.

Developing and producing reading materials for adult learners living in a variety of contexts and speaking a variety of languages is a challenging task, but experiences in several countries indicate that it can be done. In addition to materials produced at central production facilities, a variety of technologies makes it possible for communities to produce their own reading materials.

### *Evaluation of adult literacy programmes*

Evaluation identifies the reasons why the programme is or is not achieving its goals and objectives. The general purposes for regularly evaluating literacy programmes are listed below:

— To measure what has been achieved in each stage of implementation against the objectives for that stage.

— To determine whether the programme is meeting the short- and long-term educational goals of the learners.

— To learn about existing problems in order to devise appropriate solutions.

— To identify goals and objectives that need to be revised.

— To measure the results of the programme against its costs.

- To provide information for donor agencies and other stakeholders.
- To gather insights that can be shared with others.
- To assess the quality of materials that have been produced.

Evaluation of literacy programmes at each level of implementation may involve both external and internal evaluators. External evaluators bring to the process their theoretical and technical expertise, their outsider's perspective and, hopefully, a measure of objectivity. Internal evaluators are familiar with the context in which the programme takes place; they understand the relationships and the power structures; they know the local stakeholders' values and their hopes for the programme; and they are able to interpret the attitudes and behaviour of the people who are interviewed.

Evaluations provide information that can help in implementing and managing a literacy programme (formative evaluations) and information about the programme's long-term impact on individuals, groups, communities, institutions, and society in general (summative evaluations). Formative evaluations are usually conducted by internal evaluators – those, including the learners, who are involved in implementing and managing the programme. Summative evaluations are conducted at the close of a programme or after the learners have completed their course of instruction. While insiders may help plan and conduct a summative evaluation and take part in interpreting its findings, the main evaluators are usually outsiders who have not been involved in programme planning or implementation and supposedly have no stake in the evaluation results.

# 6

# Educating for a Sustainable Future

For thousands of years human societies have proved that living sustainably — as healthy and happy individuals, within caring and stable families and communities, and in harmony with the natural world — is possible. The long-term sustainability of indigenous economic and cultural systems is the result of indigenous systems of education which established a human and natural ecology totally at one with each other.

The Earth Summit in Rio de Janiero in 1992 helped educators around the world realise that education must be reoriented to once again reflect such a vision of sustainability, one that links economic well-being with cultural traditions and respect for Earth and its resources.

Almost universally value, indigenous peoples respect and love the land as a mother, treating it as sacred, believing that people, plants, animals, water, the land and the sky are all part of the same on-going cycles of life. These beliefs and the knowledge that flows from them has been passed down through the generations through a wide range of cultural practices, including direct instruction, stories, dances, ceremonies and art as well as networks of sacred places.

All are part of indigenous approaches to education that link people to the land through culture — and through culture to the land. Unfortunately, indigenous knowledge and wisdom have been undermined by the experience of colonisation, industrialisation and globalisation. By and large, indigenous priorities and systems of education have been supplanted by the somewhat narrow view that the environment and culture are valuable only in so far as they are economically productive.

The consequent disregard for the land and culture has meant that knowledge, values and skills for living sustainability have been underplayed in contemporary education.Certainly, knowledge about the Earth, its plants and animals, the functioning of ecosystems and the ways people use resources, is taught in schools and colleges in science, geography and social studies. Nature documentaries are among the more popular programmes on television while visits to museums, science centres, environmental reserves and other sites of non-formal education are expanding. However, there is a widespread problem with the way that the environment and sustainable development are presented in such formal and non-formal programmes.

Few attempts are made to link the health of people to the health and sustainability of ecosystems; and students and community members are rarely asked to reflect upon the impacts of their activities and those of their families and wider society on the functioning of ecosystems. In formal education, studies of society, the economy and the environment are usually within separate disciplines with little regard for developing practical skills for practising sustainability. For this reason, Agenda 21 called for a reorientation of education. Reorienting education towards sustainable development requires a new vision for education. Chapter 36 of Agenda 21, on *Education, Awareness and Training* states:

> 36.3. Education, including formal education, public awareness and training should be recognized as a process by which human beings and societies can reach their fullest potential. Education is critical for achieving environmental and ethical awareness, values and attitudes, skills and behaviour consistent with sustainable development and for effective public participation in decision-making. Both formal and non-formal education are indispensable to changing people's attitudes so that they have the capacity to assess and address their sustainable development concerns.

To achieve this vision, Chapter 36 called on governments, international agencies, businesses and civil society groups to:

— ensure that basic education and functional literacy for all is achieved

— make environmental and development education available to people of all ages

— integrate environmental and development concepts, including those of population, into all educational programmes, with analyses of the causes of the major problems

— involve schoolchildren in local and regional studies on environmental health, including safe drinking water, sanitation, food and the environmental and economic impacts of resource use.

Following the Earth Summit, the Commission on Sustainable Development appointed UNESCO to be its Task Manager for Chapter 36. UNESCO was to accelerate reforms of education and coordinate the activities of all stakeholders in education through a wide-ranging Work Programme. The seven objectives of the Work Programme were to:

— clarify and communicate the concept and key messages of education for sustainable development

— review national education policies and reorient formal educational systems

— incorporate education into national strategic and action plans for sustainable development

— educate to promote sustainable consumption and production patterns in all countries

— promote investments in education

— identify and share innovative practices

— raise public awareness.

Several activities were listed for each objective and those who might be responsible for each, e.g. governments, relevant United Nations bodies and/or NGOs, nominated. UNESCO's role has been to provide professional and technical support for governments of member states and to help disseminate the innovative policies, programmes and practices of education for sustainable development that were being developed by all stakeholders. UNESCO has had both internal and external roles to play in its responsibility as 'task manager'. The organization as a whole has been mobilized to address education from the perspective of sustainability and, with the endorsement of the

UNESCO's General Conference, has aligned its work according to the priorities laid down in the CSD work programme. Indeed, along with poverty eradication and the promotion and fair use of Information and Communication Technologies (ICTs), sustainable development is now seen a key theme across all UNESCO activities. UNESCO has also been a catalyst for clarifying key ideas, disseminating guiding principles, and sharing experiences across countries by convening international conferences and regional workshops, in developing.demonstration projects and sample curriculum and training materials, and in creating an international network of schools committed to the principles of peace, human rights, equity and conservation.

UNESCO is also facilitating the international Education for All (EFA) programme that aims to develop and implement national education action plans, enable capacity development in early-childhood, primary and science education, and catalyse new approaches to family education as well as citizenship, peace, multicultural and environmental education. UNESCO has also developed partnerships with many UN agencies, including UNFPA, WHO and ILO to promote population education, WHO to develop new approaches to health education, FAO to advance education in rural areas and promote food security, WHO and UNAIDS to combat the pandemic, UNICEF, UNHCR and major NGOs to assist in the reconstruction of education in crisis and post-conflict situations, and many more.

The challenge of sustainable development is a difficult and complex one, requiring new partnerships — among governments, academic and scientific communities, teachers, non-governmental organizations (NGOs), local communities and the media. All are essential to the birth of a culture of sustainability. Within governments, for example, education for sustainability is of direct concern not only to ministries of education, but also to ministries of health, environment, natural resources, planning, agriculture, commerce and others. New policies, programmes, resources and activities can be reported from almost every country, a sure and encouraging sign that education is beginning to be seen as a significant aspect of national sustainable development policies.

## Vision of Education for the 21st Century

Education for sustainable development is an emerging but dynamic concept that encompasses a new vision of education that seeks to empower people of all ages to assume responsibility for creating a sustainable future. Education will shape the world of tomorrow — it is the most effective means that society possesses for confronting the challenges of the future. Progress increasingly depends upon educated minds: upon research, invention, innovation and adaptation. Educated minds and instincts are needed not only in laboratories and research institutes, but also in every walk of life. While education is not the whole answer to every problem, in its broadest sense, education must be a vital part of all efforts to imagine and create new relations among people and to foster greater respect for the needs of the environment.

Since 1992, an international consensus has emerged that achieving sustainable development is essentially a process of learning. At major UN conferences of the 1990s, including those on human rights in Vienna (1993), population and development in Cairo (1994), small island developing states in Barbados (1994), social development in Copenhagen (1995), women in Beijing (1995), food security in Rome (1996), and human settlements in Istanbul (1996), the critical role of education was stressed. Just as we learnt to live unsustainably, we now need to learn our way out — to learn how to live sustainably. Sustainable development requires active and knowledgeable citizens and caring and informed decision makers capable of making the right choices about the complex and interrelated economic, social and environmental issues human society is facing.

To achieve this requires the broader process of social change known as social learning, or what the OECD calls 'enhancing societal capacity for the environment'. This involves not only specific education and training programmes but also the use of policy and legislation as opportunities for teaching and encouraging new forms of personal, community and corporate behaviour.

Social learning also involves reflection - often stimulated by religious leaders and the media - on the appropriateness of the mental models and assumptions that have traditionally guided thinking and behaviour. From such processes of social learning we have come to realise that sustainable development is a catalytic vision rather than a neatly defined, technical concept. Indeed, we have learnt that:

— Sustainable development is perhaps more a moral precept than a scientific concept, linked as much with notions of peace, human rights and fairness as with theories of ecology or global warning.

— While sustainable development involves the natural sciences, policy and economics, it is primarily a matter of culture: it is concerned with the values people cherish and with the ways in which we perceive our relationship with others and with the natural world.

— Sustainable development requires us to acknowledge the interdependent relationship between people and the natural environment. This interdependence means that no single social, economic, political or environmental objective be pursued to the detriment of others. The environment cannot be protected in a way that leaves half of humanity in poverty. Likewise there can be no long-term development on a depleted planet.

These principles remind us that sustainable development is grounded in four interdependent systems:

— Biophysical systems which provide the life support systems for all life, human and non-human;

— Economic systems which provide a continuing means of livelihood (jobs and money) for people;

— Social systems which provide ways for people to live together peacefully, equitably and with respect for human rights and dignity; and

— Political systems through which power is exercised fairly and democratically to make decisions about the way social and economic systems use the biophysical environment.

This holistic view supports four inter-related principles for sustainable living:

— Conservation to ensure that natural systems can continue to provide life support systems for all living things, including the resources that sustain the economic system.

— Peace and Equity to encourage people to live cooperatively and in harmony with each other and have their basic needs satisfied in a fair and equitable way.

— Appropriate Development to ensures that people can support themselves in a long-term way.

— Inappropriate development ignores the links between the economy and the other systems in the environment.

— Democracy to ensure that people have a fair and equal say over how natural, social and economic systems should be managed.

Linking social, economic, political and environmental concerns is a crucial aspect of sustainable development. Creating such links demands a deeper, more ambitious way of thinking about education, one that retains a commitment to critical analysis while fostering creativity and innovation. It demands that education promotes a system of ethics and values that is sensitive to cultural identity, multicultural dialogue, democratic decision-making and the appropriate use and management of natural resources. All countries have sought to respond to the challenge of social learning, within the limits of their resources.

Increased scientific understanding of the scale, severity and interlocking nature of sustainable development issues over the last two decades has led to heightened levels of environmental and social reporting in the mass media, public awareness of issues, and public support for environmental campaigns. Governments and their citizens now expect that schools and other institutions of social learning will help prepare young people to respond positively to the opportunities offered by wide public understanding of, and support, for sustainable development. The potential of education is enormous. Seen as social learning for sustainability, education can increase concern over unsustainable practices and increase our capacity to confront and master change. Education not only informs people, it can change them. As a means for personal enlightenment and for cultural renewal, education is not only central to sustainable development, it is humanity's best hope and most effective means in the quest to achieve sustainable development.

## Education and Sustainable Future

Education not only provides scientific and.technical skills, it also provides the motivation, justification, and social support for pursuing and applying them. For this reason, society must be deeply concerned that much of current education falls far short of what is required. Improving the quality and coverage of education and reorienting its goals to recognize the importance of sustainable development must be among society's highest priorities. Clarifying the concept of education for sustainable development was a major challenge for educators during the last decade.

The broad scope of Chapter 36 of Agenda 21 generated extensive debate over such issues as: the meanings of sustainable development in educational settings, the appropriate balance of peace, human rights, citizenship, social equity, ecological and development themes in already over-crowded curricula, and ways of integrating the humanities, the social sciences and the arts into what had up-to-now been seen and practised as a branch of science education.

Some argued that educating for sustainable development ran the risk of indoctrination while others wondered whether asking schools to take a lead in the transition to sustainable development was asking too much of teachers. These debates were compounded by the desire of many, predominantly environmental, NGOs to contribute to educational planning without the requisite understanding of how education systems work, how educational change and innovation takes place, and of relevant curriculum development, professional development and pedagogical principles. Not realising that effective educational change takes time, others were critical of governments for not acting more quickly.

The Commission on Sustainable Development assisted in overcoming the inertia of these debates by establishing priorities through a special Work Programme on education in 1996 and which was revised in 1998.Consequently, many international, regional and national initiatives have contributed to an expanded and refined understanding of the meaning of education for sustainable development. For example, Education International, the major umbrella group of teachers' unions and associations in the world, has issued a declaration and action plan to promote sustainable development through education. Similarly, statements and guidelines in support of reorienting education towards sustainable development have been issued by regional councils of Ministers of Education and/or Environment in the European Union, APEC, OAS, SADC, and the South Pacific.

Many regional strategic or action plans have been developed. A common call in all of these is the need for an integrated approach through which all government ministries (eg education, health, environment, finance, agriculture, industry and consumer affairs, etc.) collaborate in developing a shared understanding of and commitment to policies, strategies and programmes of education for sustainable development.

International conservation organisations such as WWF and IUCN are also actively promoting the integration of education into sustainable development at local community, national and eco-regional scales. In addition, many individual governments have established committees, panels, advisory councils and curriculum development projects to discuss education for sustainable development, develop policy and appropriate support structures, programmes and resources, and fund local initiatives. Indeed, the roots of education for sustainable development are firmly planted in the environmental education efforts of such groups.

Along with global education, development education, peace education, citizenship education, human rights education, and multicultural and anti-racist education that have all been significant, environmental education has been particularly significant. In its brief thirty-year history, contemporary environmental education has steadily striven towards goals and outcomes similar and comparable to those inherent in the concept of sustainability.

In the early 1970s, the emerging environmental education movement was given a powerful boost by the United Nations Conference on the Human Environment held in Stockholm in 1972, which recommended that environmental education be recognized and promoted in all countries. This recommendation led to.the launching in 1975 by UNESCO and the UN Environment Programme (UNEP) of the International Environmental Education Programme (IEEP), which continued until 1995. The influence of the IEEP —and the national and international activities that it inspired — have been widely felt and is reflected in many of the educational innovations carried out in the last two decades. That work was inspired largely by the guiding principles of environmental education laid down by the Intergovernmental Conference on Environmental Education held in Tbilisi in 1977. The vision and objectives in the Tbilisi Declaration integrated a broad spectrum of environmental, social, ethical, economic and cultural outcomes of education - all of which are central to education for sustainable development. Its basic principles were successfully translated into educational policies around the world and, with greater difficulty, into schoolroom practice in many countries.

The international community now strongly believes that we need to foster — through education — the values, behaviour and lifestyles required for a sustainable future. Education for sustainable development has come to be seen as a process of learning how to make decisions that consider the long-term future of the economy, ecology and social well-being of all communities. Building the capacity for such futures-oriented thinking is a key task of education.

This represents a new vision of education, a vision that helps students better understand the world in which they live, addressing the complexity and interconnectedness of problems such as poverty, wasteful consumption, environmental degradation, urban decay, population growth, gender inequality, health, conflict and the violation of human rights that threaten our future. This vision of education emphasises a holistic, interdisciplinary approach to developing the knowledge and skills needed for a sustainable future as well as changes in values, behaviour, and lifestyles. This requires us to reorient education systems, policies and practices in order to empower everyone, young and old, to make decisions and act in culturally appropriate and locally relevant ways to redress the problems that threaten our common future. In this way, people of all ages can become empowered to develop and evaluate alternative visions of a sustainable future and to fulfil these visions through working creatively with others. Seeking sustainable development through education requires educators to:

— place an ethic for living sustainably, based upon principles of social justice, democracy, peace and ecological integrity, at the centre of society's concerns

— encourage a meeting of disciplines, a linking of knowledge and of expertise, to create understandings that are more integrated and contextualized

— encourage lifelong learning, starting at the beginning of life and grounded in life — one based on a passion for a radical transformation of the moral character of society

— develop to the maximum the potential of all human beings throughout their lives so that they can achieve self-fulfilment and full self-expression with the collective achievement of a viable future

— value aesthetics, the creative use of the imagination, an openness to risk and flexibility, and a willingness to explore new options

— encourage new alliances between the State and civil society in promoting citizens' emancipation and the practice of democratic principles

— mobilize society in a concerted effort so as to eliminate poverty and all forms of violence and injustice

— encourage a commitment to the values for peace in such a way as to promote the creation of new lifestyles and living patterns

— identify and pursue new human projects in the context of local sustainability within a planetary consciousness and a personal and communal awareness of global responsibility.

— create realistic hope in which the possibility of change and the real desire for change are accompanied by a concerted, active participation in change, at the appropriate time, in favour of a sustainable future for all.

There are over 60 million teachers in the world - and each one is a key agent for bringing about the changes in lifestyles and systems that we need. But, education is not confined to the classrooms of formal education. As an approach to social learning, education for sustainable development also encompasses the wide range of learning activities in basic and post-basic education, technical and vocational training and tertiary education, and both non-formal and informal learning by both young people and adults within their families and workplaces and in the wider community.

Deciding how education should contribute to sustainable development is a major task. In coming to decisions about what approaches to education will be locally relevant and culturally appropriate, countries, educational institutions and their communities may take heed of the following key lessons learnt from discussion and debate about education and sustainable development over the past decade.

— Education for sustainable development must explore the economic, political and social implications of sustainability by encouraging learners to reflect critically on their own areas of the world, to identify non-viable elements in their own lives and to explore the tensions among conflicting aims.

— Development strategies suited to the particular circumstances of various cultures in the pursuit of shared development goals will be crucial. Educational approaches must take into account the experiences of indigenous cultures and minorities, acknowledging and facilitating their original and important contributions to the process of sustainable development.

— The movement towards sustainable development depends more on the development of our moral sensitivities than on the growth of our scientific understanding — important as that is. Education for sustainable development cannot be concerned only with disciplines that improve our understanding of nature, despite their undoubted value. Success in the struggle for sustainable development requires an approach to education that strengthens our engagement in support of other values and the awareness that we share a common destiny with others.

— Ethical values are the principal factor in social cohesion and, at the same time, the most effective agent of change and transformation. Ultimately, sustainability will depend on changes in behaviour and lifestyles, changes which will need to be motivated by a shift in values and rooted in the cultural and moral precepts upon which behaviour is based. Without change of this kind, even the most enlightened legislation, the cleanest technology, the most sophisticated research will not succeed in steering society towards the long-term goal of sustainability.

— Changes in lifestyle will need to be accompanied by the development of an ethical awareness, whereby the inhabitants of rich countries discover within their cultures the source of a new and active solidarity, which will make possible to eradicate the widespread poverty that now besets 80% of the world's population as well as the environmental degradation and other problems linked to it.

— Ethical values are shaped through education, in the broadest sense of the term. Education is also essential in enabling people to use their ethical values to make informed and ethical choices. Fundamental social changes, such as those required to move towards sustainability, come about either because people sense an ethical imperative to change or because leaders have the political will to lead in that direction and sense that the people will follow them.

— The effectiveness of education for sustainable development must ultimately be measured by the degree to which it changes the attitudes and behaviours of people, both in their individual roles, including those of producers and consumers, and in carrying out their collective responsibilities and duties as citizens.

## Basic Education for All

Basic education provides the foundation for all future education and learning. Its goal, as concerns those in the pre-school and primary school-age population, whether enrolled in school or not, is to produce children who are happy with themselves and with others, who find learning exciting and develop inquiring minds, who begin to build up a storehouse of knowledge about the world and, more importantly, an approach to seeking knowledge that they can use and develop throughout their lives.

Basic education is also integral to lifelong learning, especially in increasing the level adult literacy. Millions more attend only briefly — often for a year or less — then leave without the most essential elements of a basic education or the skills to make their way in an increasingly complex and knowledge-based world. These will join the nearly 900 million adults, the majority of whom are women, who cannot read. Those denied an education suffer enormous social and economic disadvantage.

They are amongst those with the poorest health, lowest housing standards, and poorest employment prospects in the world. In fact, they have less of nearly everything in life, except children. In Peru, for example, women with ten or more years of education bear an average of 2.5 children whereas women with no education have an average of 7.4 children.

In other countries, the difference is less extreme, but still sizeable. Nearly everywhere, higher levels of education — especially for girls and women — reduces the average size of families while contributing to the health, well-being and education of children. However, this is not the only way education impacts upon sustainability. Education is essential for mobilizing minds and communities in the struggle for sustainable development.

Education for All (EFA)The World Conference on Education for All (Jomtien, Thailand, 1990) marked a new start in the global quest to universalize basic education and eradicate illiteracy. The Jomtien Conference also marked the beginning of a broader vision of basic education to include, as well as literacy and numeracy, the general knowledge, skills, values and attitudes that they require to survive, develop their capacities, live and work in dignity, improve the quality of their lives, make informed decisions and continue learning.

The Education for All (EFA) Year 2000 Assessment was the end-of-decade review of the objectives agreed in Jomtien. This was the most in-depth evaluation of basic education ever undertaken. National assessments, sample surveys, case studies, a series of fourteen thematic studies, and data on eighteen statistical indicators quantified progress in more than 180 countries. The Assessment revealed that none of the EFA targets set at Jomtien were met in their entirety —most notably, the fundamental goal of achieving 'universal access to, and completion of' basic education by 2000'. However, many successes were noted:

— The number of children enrolled in school rose from an estimated 599 million in 1990 to 681 million in 1998, nearly twice the average increase during the preceding decade. Eastern Asia and the Pacific, as well as Latin America and the Caribbean are now close to, and China and India have made substantial progress towards, achieving universal primary education. Developing.countries as a whole have achieved a net-enrolment ratio in primary education in excess of 80 per cent.

— The importance of early childhood education is now recognised, and the idea that education begins at birth has taken root in many societies. As a result, the number of children in pre-school education rose by 5 per cent in the past decade.

— More people are now entering secondary education and the rate of completion for upper secondary education is rising steeply with each successive age group. Worldwide, secondary education enrolment has expanded ten-fold over the past fifty years, from 40 million in 1950 to more than 400 million today. Over the same period, tertiary education enrolments increased nearly fourteen fold from 6.5 million in 1950 to 88.2 million in 1997.

— The number of literate adults grew significantly over the past decade, from an estimated 2.7 billion in 1990 to 3.3 billion in 1998. The overall global adult literacy rate now stands at 85 per cent for men, 74 per cent for women. More than 50% of the world's adult population has now attended primary school.

However, an estimated 880 million adults cannot read or write, and in the least developed countries one out of every two individuals falls into this category. Two-thirds of illiterate adults are women — exactly the same proportion as ten years ago.

— A few countries have made progress in reducing inequalities of educational opportunity as reflected by gender, disability, ethnicity, urban versus rural location and working children.

Positive trends in primary education mask disparity of access both between and within many countries, and disparities in educational quality can remain even when access rates are high. People in poor, rural and remote communities, ethnic minorities and indigenous populations have shown little or no progress over the past decade. And the gender gap persists. Despite the concerns noted, these improvements represent a substantial contribution to building capacity for sustainable development.

In 2000, ten years after Jomtien, the World Education Forum (Dakar, Senegal) confirmed the World Declaration on Education for All, and agreed to six new goals in the Dakar Framework for Action

— To expand and improve comprehensive early childhood care and education, especially for the most vulnerable and disadvantaged children;

— To ensure that by 2015 all children, particularly girls, children in difficult circumstances and those belonging to ethnic minorities, have access to and complete free and compulsory primary education of good quality;

— To ensure that the learning needs of all young people are met through equitable access to appropriate learning and life skills programmes;

— To achieve a 50 per cent improvement in levels of adult literacy by 2015, especially for women as well as equitable access to basic and continuing education for adults;

— To eliminate gender disparities in primary and secondary education by 2005 and achieve gender equality by 2015 with a focus on ensuring full and equal access to and achievement in basic education of good quality;

— To improve all aspects of the quality of education and ensure excellence of all, so that recognized and measurable learning outcomes are achieved by all, especially in literacy, numeracy and essential life skills.

These goals make the links between basic education and sustainable development very clear. Indeed, the Dakar Framework for Action states, 'Education is ... the key to sustainable development and peace and stability with and among countries, and thus an indispensable means for effective participation in the societies and economies of the twenty-first century'

UNESCO was nominated to orchestrate global efforts to achieve EFA by 2015, and is building partnerships with governments, civil society groups, regional organisations and international agencies. A key component of this is the International Decade For Literacy which strongly links education to the crucial task of poverty alleviation.

The following principles learned from successful EFA activities over the past decade are being integrated into regional and national EFA action plans:

— EFA goals are attainable provided that the problems of educational access are addressed first and adequately.

— Redressing inequalities and disparities in access, quality and learning outcomes should be the cornerstone of national educational policy-making, planning and implementation

— Increased attention should be given to curriculum planning and the provision of adequate and relevant learning materials for improved teaching and learning processes.

— The content of education, as well as processes of teaching and learning, need to be more learner-centred and less controlled by syllabuses, textbooks and examination requirements. This makes the school curriculum relevant, and also helps students become self-motivators, self-learners and critical thinkers.

— School effectiveness and learning outcomes can be improved through developing a culture of maintenance, discipline, stewardship, care and self-esteem, democratic management, school-community partnerships, and a commitment to responsibility, professionalism and excellence.

— The home environment has a major impact on learning outcomes. Parental education and home learning support are vital to learners, providing health and nutrition, moral values and codes of conduct, positive attitudes to education, and support for the school's requirements of learners.

— Systematic and continuous assessment, monitoring and evaluation schemes are needed to understand the dynamics of educational change and to help stakeholders develop appropriate responses.

A special audience of basic education are the millions of young people and adults living in emergency and post-conflict situations where the education system has been destabilised, disorganised or destroyed due to human-made crises such as civil strife and war or natural disasters such as flood and drought. The number of such people is not inconsiderable. At the end of 1999, the UNHCR recognised that there were over 15 million refugees in the world;other estimates placed the number of internally displaced persons at between 20 million and 50 million.These data mean that up to one per cent of the world's population has been displaced by conflict or other disasters, have returned home under difficult circumstances, or are otherwise attempting to rebuild their lives and communities without access to services such as education.

However, education is a vital way for students, their families and their communities to begin the trauma healing process, and to learn the skills and values needed for a more peaceful future and better governance at local and national levels. At its most basic level, this is education for sustainable development. Key lessons for education in emergency situations have been identified by UNHCR and its partners in the Interagency Network Group for Education in Emergencies , including:

— A rapid response to educational reconstruction is vital.

— A community-based approach, e.g. through the involvement of local groups in conducting needs and skills assessments, can ensure high levels of participation in education.

— Existing capacity should be strengthened through providing resources and training for teacher, youth leaders and school management committees

— Attention needs to be paid to the emotional and physical needs of learners as well as cognitive ones, particularly focusing on the needs of special groups, such as the physically maimed or abused, mentally traumatised, former child soldiers, etc.

— Durable educational solutions are most often related to the curriculum and language of study in the country of origin, and should provide physical and social protection skills, sustain study skills, and develop survival and peace-building messages and skills..

## Reorientation of Education Policies

To be an effective change agent, the fundamental purposes of education have to change. The current challenge is not so much to reorient education, but to collectively learn to change our perceptions about the purpose and role of education towards a systems based and sustainability oriented paradigm. Without a change in values, technical measure to promote education for sustainable development will have little effect. Ten years after the Rio Conference, there is substantial progress towards the reorientation of educational systems in terms of how to prepare people for life: for job security; for the demands of a rapidly changing society; for technological changes that now directly or indirectly affect every part of life; and, ultimately, for the quest for happiness, well-being and quality of life.

Globalisation is proving to be a particular challenge to education. Its economic impacts have been uneven and its cultural impacts threaten local ways of viewing the world. However, globalisation has brought an awareness of the scale of the shared burdens we face and of ways of cooperating with others to address them. Within many countries, formal education systems that were no longer considered adequate to meet the needs of society and the workplace have been rethought. For the most part, however, the limited achievements serve only to show the new direction in which curriculum reform needs to move. Nevertheless, core themes and key lessons for reorienting education policies, programme and practices towards sustainable development can be identified. These include: a balanced and holistic range of objectives, interdisciplinarity, student-centred learning, and an emphasis on futures education, citizenship education, education for a culture of peace, gender equality and respect for human rights, population education, health education, education for protecting and managing the natural resource base of economic and social development, and education for sustainable consumption.

While education reproduces certain aspects of current society, it also prepares students to transform society for the future. Education must help students to determine what is best conserved in their cultural, economic and natural heritage. It must also nurture values and strategies for attaining sustainability locally, nationally and globally. This requires a curriculum that enhances life skills as a foundation for basic education, as set out in the Dakar Framework for Action, and that balances knowledge, values and skills objectives.

Reorienting education for sustainable development encompasses a vision for society that is not only ecologically sustainable but also one which is socially, economically and politically sustainable as well. To achieve this vision, schools should plan learning experiences that enable students to achieve the following objectives:

1) Skills: The ability to engage in:
   - Critical and creative thinking
   - Oral, written and graphic communication
   - Collaboration and cooperation
   - Conflict management
   - Decision making, problem solving and planning
   - Using appropriate technology, media and ICTs
   - Civic participation and action
   - Evaluation and reflection
2) Attitudes and values
   - Respecting Earth and life in all its diversity;
   - Caring for the community of life – both human and non-human - with understanding, compassion and love;
   - Building democratic societies that are just, sustainable, participatory and peaceful; and
   - Securing Earth's bounty and beauty for present and future generations.
3) *Knowledge:* An understanding of, and ability to apply the concepts of:

— *Sustainable development*: A process by which the needs of present generations can be satisfied without compromising the ability of future generations to satisfy their needs.

— *Interdependence*: The relationships of mutual dependence between all elements and life forms, including humans, within natural systems.

— *Basic human needs*: The needs and right of all people and societies for fair and equitable access to flows of energy and materials for survival and a satisfying quality of life within the limits of the Earth.

— *Human rights:* The fundamental freedoms of conscience and religion, expression, peaceful assembly and association, which ensure access to democratic participation and meeting basic human needs.

— *Democracy*: The right of all people to access channels for community decision making.

— *Local-global links*: The recognition that the consumption of a product or service in one part of the world is dependent on flows of energy and materials in other parts of the world and that this creates potential opportunities and losses economically, socially and environmentally at all points in the local-global chain.

— *Biodiversity*: The diverse and interdependent composition of life forms in an ecosystem that is necessary for sustaining flows of energy and materials indefinitely.

— *Interspecies equity*: A consideration of the need for humans to treat creatures decently, and protect them from cruelty and avoidable suffering.

— *Ecological footprint*: The area of land and water needed to support the total flow of energy and materials consumed by a community or population indefinitely.

— *Precautionary principle*: The need to act judiciously and with an awareness of unintended consequences when we do not possess all the facts on a situation and/or when scientific advice on an issue is divided.

Reorienting education to sustainability requires us to work increasingly at the interface of disciplines in order to address the complex problems of today's world. What people will need to know in five, ten, twenty or fifty years cannot be reliably predicted. It is predictable, however, that such developments will not fit neatly into the disciplinary boundaries that have been in place for more than a century. Hence, understanding and solving complex problems is likely to require intensified co-operation among scientific fields as well as between the pure and mathematical sciences and the social sciences, the arts and the humanities. Reorienting education to sustainable development will, in short, require important, even dramatic changes, in the way we think of knowledge.

Participation in the decisions that affect their lives is a key element in the Convention on the Rights of the Child. Learning how to participate requires that children and young people have opportunities, within the safety of a learning environment, to practice decision-making. This may be done through curriculum and assessment policies that encourage the development of self-esteem and personal responsibility and of skills for learning how to learn, for critical thinking, and for active participation. Space needs to be left in the curriculum for students to plan their own learning goals and methods, as and when appropriate, and for self- and peer-assessment. Resource-based teaching, enquiry and discovery learning, values clarification and analysis, problem-based learning, simulation games and role play, and learning through community problem solving are student-centred approaches to learning that need to be encouraged. Such approaches encourage authentic or 'deep learning' rather than the 'shallow learning' of rote recall and memorisation for examinations.

Authentic learning relates to everyday issues and future concerns. It proceeds at the pace at which individuals learn well rather than by imposed schedules and standards. Authentic education engages the 'whole person' — body, mind and spirit — in the learning process and creates enthusiasm, insight and reflection as well as compassion, energy and a commitment to working individually and with others to build a sustainable future.Futures Education If it is true that all education is for the future then the future needs to become a more explicit element in all levels of education.

As education for sustainable development is education for a future that we cannot yet predict, it is important that education programmes seek to develop skills for understanding and anticipating change and for facing the future with courage and hope. This would involve coming to realise.that the future is a human creation, made by our decisions, and that in a democratic society, people have the right, indeed an obligation, to contribute positively to a sustainable future. This would involve learning how to learn, how to analyse and solve complex problems, how to think creatively and critically about the future, how to anticipate and make our own histories.

### *Concerns of Gender Equaltiy*

Women are the primary care-givers and the managers of natural resources, including food, shelter and consumption of goods, in most cultures. In addition, women also have jobs and careers. However, the general failure to provide equal opportunities for women to pursue education and economic self-sufficiency has meant that a disproportionate number of women are poor and marginalised. These social barriers - exclusion, low status and poverty - are also barriers to a sustainable future. These facts make the education of girls and women a priority for sustainable development. It also means that all people, male and female, need to learn about the issues of gender and sustainable development and to learn within environments that are sensitive to the learning needs and styles of both males and females.

Curriculum materials aimed at promoting such understanding are being produced in most countries. Education systems and schools are also developing policies that promote gender equality within educational processes while teacher education programmes are drawing attention to the importance of including a gender perspective in all subject areas. UNESCO, national governments and many organizations are also seeking to advance the participation of girls in science, mathematics and information and communication technologies. These are important beginnings in the process of promoting gender equality in and through education.

### *Education: Integrate Citizenship Objectives*

Around the world, efforts are being made to integrate citizenship objectives into the formal curriculum. This has involved the promotion of content themes as well as teaching, learning and assessment processes that emphasize values, ethical motivation and the ability to work with others to help build a sustainable future. The global spread of democracy has expanded electoral enfranchisement and meant that adult education for citizenship is also expanding A key aspect of citizenship education within the context of sustainable development is international understanding. This helps bring an understanding of the links between local and global issues. It also means that young people can be given opportunities to examine their own cultural values and beliefs, to appreciate the similarities between peoples everywhere, to understand the global contexts of their lives, and to develop skills that will enable them to combat prejudice and discrimination. In these ways, students can use their knowledge, skills and commitments to plan an active role in the global community.

### *Importance of Human Rights Education*

A key pillar of education is learning how to live together in peace and harmony. This involves, firstly, strengthening one's own identify, self-worth and self-confidence and, then, learning to appreciate the cultures of others, to respect others as individuals and groups, and to apply the same ethical principles to decisions about other people that one would apply within one's own culture. These are key learnings for life in the 21st Century..Yet, schools are sometimes affected by deep-seated national stereotypes of others, overly nationalistic sentiments and views of history, and contemporary ethnic, religious and political tensions. Schools can even pass on partisan views inadvertently, for example through insensitively written or out-dated textbooks. The UNESCO Associated Schools Project (ASP-NET) has been instrumental in developing strategies and resources for promoting human rights and peace in the curriculum.

### *Importance of Health Education*

A child's ability to attain her or his full potential is directly related to the synergistic effect of good health, good nutrition and appropriate education. Good health and good education are not only ends in themselves, but also means which provide individuals with the chance to lead productive and satisfying lives. School health is an investment in a country's future and in the capacity of its people to thrive economically and as a society. Thus, good health and nutrition are both essential inputs and important outcomes of basic education. Children must be healthy and well-nourished in order to fully participate in education and gain its maximum benefits.

Early childhood care programmes and primary schools that improve children's health and nutrition can enhance the learning and educational outcomes of school children, especially girls, and thus for the next generation of children as well. In addition, a healthy, safe and secure school environment can help protect children from health hazards, abuse and exclusion. Improving the health and learning of school children through school-based health and nutrition programmes is not a new concept.

Many countries have school health programmes, and many agencies have decades of experience. These common experiences suggest an opportunity for concerted action by a partnership of agencies to broaden the scope of school health programmes and make them more effective. Thus, WHO, UNICEF, UNESCO and the World Bank have developed a.core group of cost effective strategies for making schools healthy for children and so contribute to the development of child-friendly schools. These agencies have launched a new approach to health education called FRESH (Focusing Resources on Effective School Health). The FRESH framework is a starting point for developing an effective school health component in broader efforts to achieve more child-friendly schools. The FRESH framework involves four components:

— Health-related school policies, including skills-based health education and the provision of some health services, can help promote the overall health, hygiene and nutrition of children.

— Provision of safe water and sanitation can ensure that all schools have access to clean water and sanitation. By providing these facilities, schools can reinforce the health and hygiene messages, and act as an example to both students and the wider community.

— Skills-based health education focuses upon the development of knowledge, attitudes, values, and life skills needed to make and act on the most appropriate and positive health-related decisions

— School-based health and sanitation services can deliver vital health and nutritional services if they are simple, safe and familiar, and address problems that are prevalent and recognised as important within the community.

At the beginning of the 21st century, the education of many children and young people around the world is compromised by conditions and behaviours that undermine their physical and emotional well-being. Hunger, malnutrition, malaria, polio and intestinal infections, drug and alcohol abuse, violence and injury, unplanned pregnancy, HIV/AIDS and other sexually transmitted infections are some of the health problems faced. As a result, schools must be not only centres for academic learning, but also supportive venues for the provision of essential health education and services.

HIV/AIDS is a major concern for teachers and education systems. The impacts on people's lives —and on the opportunities for economic activities — mean that the epidemic is a major threat to plans for a sustainable future. The experience of UNESCO, UNICEF, WHO and others indicate several key lessons for effective school-based preventive education programmes, including:

— HIV-related issues need to be integrated into broader education about reproductive health, life skills, substance use, and other health issues.

— Prevention and health programmes should not only teach young people the biomedical aspects of reproductive health but they should also learn how to cope with the complex demands of relationships.

— Programmes that adopt a life skills approach are most successful; these help young people take greater control of their lives by making healthy life choices, gaining greater resistance to negative pressures, and minimising harmful behaviours.

— Prevention and health programmes should begin at the earliest possible age and certainly before sexual activity.

— Prevention and health programmes should extend to the whole educational setting, including the school system, students, teachers and other school personnel, parents, and the community around the school.

UNESCO is currently investigating how education systems need to adapt to the new contexts that are resulting from the pandemic as a way of illustrating that the quality of education that students receive is vital to their personal and social futures.

### *Importance of Population Education*

Sustainable development requires new ways of thinking and acting. Within this context, the relationship between education and population needs to be seen in the broader context of the struggle to overcome poverty, promote justice and equity and ensure respect of the environment and for the right of future generations to live healthy and fulfilling lives. Population education is aimed at enabling learners to better understand the nature, causes and effects of population dynamics and the manner in which they affect — and, in turn, are affected by — the actions of individuals, families, communities and nations. Properly conducted, population education is liberating and empowering, not indoctrination or propaganda. It does not seek to impose particular attitudes or behaviours upon learners, but rather to enable them to make informed decisions that serve their own best interest. The key lessons learnt about population education over the last decade include:

— Education can be consciously used to achieve population and health objectives. Increasing general levels of education is, over time, a highly effective means of dealing with population issues. Specific programmes, however, are needed to focus on urgent problems, such as HIV/AIDS, or vulnerable groups, such as poor women in developing countries.

— Population education must deal with values and views. Clarifying and classifying these is especially important in the emotionally charged issues of sex and reproduction confronted by young adults, particularly young women. The goal is to teach people to think and reason for themselves, to develop self-respect as well as respect for others, to think ahead and plan their future, and to carefully consider the implications as well as the consequences of their behaviour on themselves and others.

— A considerable number of population education programmes have been addressed specifically to girls and young women. They also, where necessary, provide referrals to health services. Many studies show that girls and women suffer from lower self-esteem and expectations than do boys or men in similar situations. Population education programmes, when well conceived and executed, can become lead a school's response to these problems.

— Women cannot adequately protect their sexual and reproductive health in the context of power imbalances with their male partners. Thus, many population initiatives are also beginning to provide boys with caring, informed, and responsible images of what it means to be 'male'. This has given rise to a range of programmes to collect information on and support the preparation of boys for effective fatherhood, responsible masculinity, more equal participation in decision-making about contraception and fertility, and fuller participation in caring for children.

— Probably no single factor is as important to the success of population education as the training and motivation of teachers. Teacher training colleges are a strategic entry point for introducing needed population education information and, more importantly, for providing training in the communication skills, attitudes, and approaches that a subject dealing with intimate behaviours requires.

— The prevailing attitudes and practices within schools are also important in either strengthening or undermining the messages of population education. Discussion of gender equality, for example, is pointless where the school itself limits the opportunities available to girls to participate equally in all fields of study and activities.

Successful population education programmes share a number of common characteristics. They appear to be well adapted to their socio-economic conditions and institutional structures; they provide coherent, easy to understand and convincing messages; they make use of well-trained teachers; and they enjoy the unequivocal support of the education system and its leaders.

### *Education for Developing Job Skills*

Parents around the world are rightly keen that their children should do well at school and then get a job. However, job opportunities are increasingly difficult to find, especially in rapidly changing.economies. Most students will make their living at home, in villages, on farms, working with their families using the resources of their local environment or in the informal or 'popular' economies of cities. Those who continue to higher levels of schooling may find employment in the formal sector, but will still need knowledge and skills so they can help their communities make informed decisions.

Core concepts and skills in Language, Maths, Science and Social Science are important, but practical skills for earning a living are also vital. Lack of appropriate preparation for work in local villages and communities has contributed to rural-urban drift and, in the long run, to high rates of unemployment, poverty and crime in cities in many countries. Meeting the needs of sustainable livelihoods, not just of the formal economy and workplace, calls for an approach to education that would equip young people with basic skills to take control of their own lives, to improve their standard of living, and to make decisions about development that is appropriate to their own communities, both urban and rural. The new syllabus is being introduced into the core curriculum in Papua New Guinea to integrate these important life and vocational skills into basic education.

### *Education for Protecting Natural Resources*

Education in all its forms is making a major contribution to protecting ecosystems and integrating natural resource management and energy conservation, through promoting awareness, knowledge, skills, values and action objectives. Biodiversity education is well served by the many NGOs concerned for local and global ecosystems.

Educators in botanic gardens, museums and other non-formal learning centres have made especially important contributions, as have television documentaries and the media in general. However, a minority of these remain restricted to a narrow, nature-based environmental education approach. Many energy producers have developed energy education programmes that integrate social and environmental issues into broader lessons about the physics of electricity, alternative and renewable energy sources, and the importance of energy conservation.

Of all natural resources, water is the most precious, and hence water must be a significant theme in education for sustainable development. Governments, water authorities, conservation NGOs and community organisations have all played prominent roles in establishing action-oriented water quality monitoring projects that link schools with their local communities and environment.

Programmes with names such as Global Rivers Environmental Education Network (GREEN), Waterwatch, Streamwatch, Ribbons of Blue, the Schools Water Action Project (SWAP), Springs Project, etc., as well as coastal and maritime programmes such as Coastwatch, Coastcare, Adopt-A-Beach, Baltic Seas Project, etc. have successfully generated concern and action for a sustainable future.

Indeed, among the most successful programmes are those that avoid the belief that awareness leads to understanding, understanding leads to concern, and concern motivates the development of skills and action. Instead, the key ingredient of success is to start from the questions, issues and problems that concern young people, themselves, and to help them develop 'action competence' through community-based learning.

Action competence brings the capacity to envision alternatives, clarify the values and interests that underlie different visions, and make choices between visions. This includes developing the skills to plan, take action and evaluate needed in active and informed citizens. Action competence brings knowledge, not just of the problem and its symptoms but also about its root causes — how it impacts on people's lives, ways of addressing it, and how different interests are served by different sorts of solutions.

Consumption lies at the heart of the debate about sustainable development as it covers people's right to live and work in a clean environment with good health and social conditions. However, what counts as sustainable consumption and a sustainable lifestyle depends on context and culture. For example, in the North major changes are needed to reduce the impacts of consumption, whereas in the South, consumption levels may need to rise in the interests of global equality — otherwise, the basic human needs for food, water, housing, education, health and transport for the 4.4 billion people who live in the South may not be met.

One of the tasks of education for sustainable development, especially in Northern countries, is to explain why these differences exist and the many ways in which the social and environmental impacts of their consumption pasterns may be reduced with very little, if any, decline in one's quality of life. Education programmes need to integrate sustainable consumption issues so that young people can determine an appropriate balance between their rights as consumers and their responsibilities as citizens. Such programmes must not only change attitudes and values but also develop action competence, the ability to act in democratic and thoughtful ways to bring about change. Such programmes need to be based on at least three key principles:

— Programmes that provide information on environmental facts and the need to change, or try to tell people how to behave, are generally ineffective.

— Programmes should provide understanding on why particular changes are important, and helping people explore a range of alternatives in order to find ones that make sense in their own lives.

— Programmes should provide opportunities for people to develop and practise skills such as problem solving and decision making.

## *Education for Rural Development*

The problems of poverty and deprivation in rural areas and their spill-over into urban areas cannot be solved by preventing urbanisation and keeping rural people confined to rural areas — which would be impossible in any event. The challenge of education to serve rural transformation must become one of the main themes of the Education for All effort. Not taking up this challenge is to imperil the total education for all effort.

In spite of rapid urbanization, three billion or 60 per cent of the people in developing countries, and half of the people of the world, still live in rural areas. Three quarters of the world's poor, those earning less than a dollar a day, live in rural areas. One in five children in the South still does not attend primary school and, while rural-urban statistics on education are scarce, many countries report that non-attendance in school, early dropout of students, adult illiteracy and gender inequality in education are disproportionately high in rural areas, as is poverty. Urban-rural disparities in educational investment and in the quality of teaching and learning are also widespread.

Rural people and rural areas are not homogeneous, and so for education to be relevant, it needs to respond to the diversity of rural situations. Educational activities have to be linked to the specific needs of the rural community for skills and capacities to seize economic opportunities, improve livelihood and enhance the quality of life. A multi-sectorial educational approach involving all ages and formal, non-formal and informal education is necessary. These concerns are being taken up in the FAO/UNESCO EFA Flagship Programme on Education for Rural People.

In the rural context, early childhood education can compensate, at least partially, for the disadvantages of poverty in the home and family environment. While delivery mechanisms will differ from context to context, essentially, any early childhood programme designed for rural communities must encompass:

— the provision of specially trained care and education providers who are child-friendly and child-sensitive and as far as possible, belong to the community or village in which the programme is based.

— a learning environment, teaching methods and classroom materials that are stimulating and invigorating to attract the child as well as hold her attention

— health and nutrition components that monitor both physical and mental growth as well as curative inputs and meal supplements to help improve nutrition levels of children

— counselling and information dissemination for parents on child rearing, nutrition, health and education.

To achieve social and economic development in rural areas, rural education needs to be planned as an integrated package of traditional ways of knowing, academic knowledge, and practical skills. It is also important that school curricula support the development of practical skills for earning a living in the rural economy. Thus, the curriculum needs to focus upon such topics and themes as:

— farm planning and management, rational decision-making, record keeping, cost and revenue computations, and use of credit

— application of improved farm practices

— storage, processing and food preservation

— supplementary skills for farm maintenance and improvement, as well as sideline jobs for extra income

— knowledge of government services, policies, programs, etc.

— knowledge and skills for family improvement (e.g. health, nutrition, home economics, child care, family planning) and civic skills (e.g. knowledge of how co-operatives, local government, national government function)

— new and improved technical skills applicable to particular goods and services

— management skills (business planning; record keeping and cost accounting; procurement and inventory control; market analysis and sales methods; customer and employee relations; knowledge of government services, regulations, taxes; use of credit)

— leadership skill for generating community enthusiasm and collective action, staff team work and support from higher echelons.

In community learning centres, ongoing programmes are needed to upgrade and refine existing skills and teach fresh skills that help the rural community to link with new, evolving markets in surrounding urban areas. To design a programme to meet the community's needs, surveys must first assess existing levels and categories of skills and also the demands of local and neighbouring markets. Then, school learning centres need trained instructors who impart hands-on instructions of sufficient duration and levels of sophistication. Simultaneously, sufficient quantities of raw materials and sets of machinery and tools have to be provided.

Vocational and skill development programmes are most effective when they are linked to locally functioning small industries or co-operatives or to nearby units that can provide much-needed expertise and then use the skills that are taught by employing those they have helped to train. Some countries have gone even further and have located at district levels centrally funded institutions that have the financial and technical resources to facilitate and assist skill development programmes run by community learning centres.

Lifelong learning is at the heart of transformation of the rural community, and must ideally develop and enrich the minds of community members. This is possible only if people have access to attractive and user-friendly reading rooms and library facilities. Managers of continuing education projects need to ensure that reading rooms and libraries are conveniently located, accessible to all members of the.community, and well stocked with books and periodicals that balance the requirements for knowledge or information on the one hand and pure entertainment on the other. If cyber kiosks can rapidly dot the urban landscape, there is no reason why rural communities cannot have their libraries/information centres equipped with television and internet facilities.

Literacy is an essential skills for coping with the economic and social changes that are rapidly affecting traditional rural ways of living. Literacy and continuing education projects are needed to help rural people understand the 'what' and the 'how' of production and the marketing of goods and services. They can develop and upgrade the skills needed to improve land productivity and to assist members of rural society relate to new technologies and respond creatively to new income and earning opportunities.

Lifelong learning, including adult and community education, appropriate technical and vocational education, higher education and teacher education are vital ingredients of capacity building for a sustainable future. Lifelong learning will hold the key to ensuring that, with the further development of information and communication technology, we avoid the 'have' and the 'have-nots' of the past. At the same time, we must ensure that we use the talent of all, to fulfil the potential of individuals and to ensure our economic survival as a nation. Lifelong learning is also essential to sustaining a civilised and cohesive society, in which people can develop as active citizens, where creativity is fostered and communities can be given practical support to overcome generations of disadvantage.

Sustainable development requires that education not only continue throughout life, but be as broad as life itself also; that is, it is an approach to education that serves all people, draws upon all domains of knowledge, and seeks to integrate learning into all of life's major activities. The time when education was the activity of childhood and work the pursuit of adults is long over.

Education, at all levels, is a continual process in which instruction is offered to people at every stage of life — formally and informally by different systems. The foundation of lifelong learning is basic education which extends beyond pre-school, primary and junior secondary schooling, to include basic literacy education for adults who may have missed important educational opportunities earlier in life. Only by taking this view will we successfully include the excluded, and reach those who otherwise could not be reached. The rapid growth of knowledge has rendered the notion of schooling as a 'once and for all' preparation for life utterly obsolete.

Knowledge is advancing exponentially, yet not nearly as fast as the need for understanding and solutions. The G8 Summit held in Cologne in 1999 issued a charter for lifelong learning. The charter argues that the challenge of globalisation is for every country to become a learning society and to ensure that its citizens are equipped with the knowledge; skills and qualifications they need, not just for improved living standards but also an improved quality of life. Economies and societies are increasing becoming knowledge based; therefore, education and skills are indispensable to economic success, social cohesion and civic responsibility. Lifelong learning can include aspects of basic education, but also adult and community education, appropriate technical and vocational education, higher education and teacher education, all vital ingredients of capacity building for a sustainable future..Adult and Community Education Action towards sustainable development ultimately depends on public awareness, understanding and support.

In democratic societies, public policy responds to the will of the people. It is here that public awareness and understanding of the need for sustainable development best expresses itself through support for laws, regulations and policies favourable to the environment. People express their preferences as they decide how to spend their money, as well as through the ballot. Public action, through voting or otherwise, is contingent on more than 'public awareness'. What is needed is an understanding of the issues, and of the likely consequences of a given purchasing or electoral decision. Public understanding is the foundation for people to fulfil their roles as responsible citizens, consumers and public-spirited individuals. Public awareness and understanding are, at once, consequences of education and influences on the educational process.

A public well informed of the need for sustainable development will insist that public educational institutions include in their curricula the scientific and other subject matters needed to enable people to participate effectively in activities directed towards achieving sustainable development. The students that emerge from such courses will, for their part, be alert to the need for public authorities to make adequate provision for the protection of the environment in all development plans. Two key lessons of adult and community education are very relevant to education for sustainable development.

First, women are most often the first to notice sustainable development problems. They see them, for example, in their local communities, in the quality of drinking water, in declining soil productivity and in their children's health. The actions of women are also often the most vital in addressing these problems. This essential relationship between gender and sustainable development means that the education of girls and women must lie at the core of education for a sustainable future.

Second, and most often following the first, is the realisation that people are not unaware of the social and environmental problems they face. In fact, more often than not, people have learnt quite a lot about them — from the media, social movements, scientists, governments and, most importantly, their daily experience. Consequently, there is a need to move beyond awareness raising, and to engage people critically and creatively in their own communities, planning and engaging in action for socially just and ecologically sound development at the local level.

The precautionary principle tells us that a major reason for focusing on adult education for sustainable development is that it would be unwise to wait for the present generation of school and college students to grow up and begin applying what they are learning. Indeed, it is today's adults who are the primary voters, consumers, workers, teachers, scientists, and parents. At the Conference on Adult Education (CONFINTEA V), meeting in Hamburg in 1997, members of the International Council for Adult Education's Learning for Environmental Action program said today's adults: 'must have the opportunity to develop their critical thinking skills, and to use their ideas, knowledge, power and imaginations to begin to make change rather than simply maintaining the ecological status quo.'

Technical and Vocational Education (TVE) is vital to two of the most urgent human resource problems facing global society: the need to develop appropriate skills for sustainable development; and the high levels of unemployment and under-employment in many countries. TVE trains technicians, who are the interface of nature, technology, economy and society and have a key role to play in helping society resolve environmental and development issues. Challenges such as: reorienting technology and managing risks, meeting essential needs such as food, water, sanitation and at the same time conserving natural resources, reducing energy and resource consumption, and many more will have to be tackled by them. Technicians, who are aware of, and have acquired practical skills for sustainable development, can ultimately apply more sustainable practices, as they are the ones who are involved in production.

Recognising the crucial role of TVE graduates in devising and implementing practical solutions to problems such as environmental degradation, the UNESCO International Congress on Technical and Vocational Education stressed that TVE systems should not only focus on economic dimensions but should also incorporate emerging issues such as use of environmentally sound technology. Formal programmes of TVE are important in countries of both the North and the South. However, non-formal TVE is also important as a strategy for empowering out-of-school youth, the homeless, street children and other marginalised youth.

Current education systems are sometimes not serving the best interests of such young people. Programmes are needed to develop practical and entrepreneurial skills in area such as recycling, alternative energy technologies, and handicrafts that can stimulate and support young people to apply their creativity, skills, and solidarity in income-generating activities, especially in the so-called informal or 'popular' economy.

The popular economy has become the main vector for productive activity for the majority of the world's poor, especially those living in the world's rapidly expanding cities. The popular economy represents the last resort against extreme poverty, youth unemployment and social exclusion, and is made up of a multitude of small businesses, often family-run, but also of individual activities run by women and youth. Jobs vary greatly, and include: recycling discarded household equipment, repairing machines, sewing, selling and transporting water, making craft goods, and market stalls.

Successful training initiatives for participation by marginalized youth in the popular economy have at least three principles in common:

— They reflect the dynamism and flexibility of the neighbourhoods, the young people, and the organisations that support them. This requires flexibility on the part of authorities that regulate the economy to develop policies that encourage, rather than hinder, small-scale local entrepreneurial activities.

— Programmes seek to develop the 'whole person' rather than just their knowledge and skills or their potential to earn a living. They also provide activities and support structures that encourage self-esteem, basic life skills (saving, credit, etc), self-protection strategies (from violence, sexual abuse and HIV/AIDS), and electoral enfranchisement.

— Partnerships are needed, especially with local schools and other educational institutions, to provide out-of-hours literacy and basic education classes and flexible examination systems to enable young people to find alternative pathways back into formal education..Higher Education Higher education has an crucial role to play in sustainable development. In the decade since the Earth Summit, many higher education institutions worldwide have made significant efforts to incorporate sustainable development into academic programmes, research, community outreach and their own management operations.

As students arrive at the university from secondary schools with experience in and a taste for interdisciplinary work, universities in many countries are slowly adapting to meet their needs and demands. Major research projects, such as that on climate change, work across disciplines. However, the frontiers between academic disciplines remain staunchly defended by professional bodies, career structures and criteria for promotion and advancement. Some progress has been made but much more remains to be done to break down disciplinary barriers and develop student — and staff — expertise in working collaboratively on real world problems in real world settings. Universities can also render a valuable service by integrating components of sustainable development into their outreach programmes for teachers, senior managers and local leaders such as mayors, parliamentarians and others in leadership positions. They can also play a key role in international co-operation and, perhaps, could do so more effectively it they gave fuller consideration to North-South research partnerships to conduct interdisciplinary inquiries into environment and development issues.

National partnering and networking has proven to be successful in sharing examples and lessons of good practice and encouraging their adoption by others. Of significance is the formation of a Global Higher Education for Sustainability Partnership (GHESP) by CRE-COPERICUS, University Leaders for a Sustainable Future, International Association of Universities and UNESCO.The objectives of GHESP include:

— To promote better understanding of, and more effective implementation of, strategies for the incorporation of sustainability in universities and other higher education institutions, beginning with signatories to the charters and declarations sponsored by the partner organizations.

— To undertake a global review and assessment of progress in making sustainability central to curriculum, research, outreach and operations in institutions of higher education, and, in so doing, assist UNESCO in its role within the UN system in contributing to the preparation of Rio + 10, as well as contribute to the follow-up of the World Conference on Higher Education.

— To identify and share effective strategies, models and best practices for promoting higher education for sustainability; and analyze experience thus far, with a view to making recommendations based on these studies in consultation with key stakeholders from both North and South, including business, governments, other UN bodies such as the United Nations University (UNU), as well as other relevant non governmental organizations.

Key lessons for success in implementing innovative policies and practices that achieve sustainable outcomes in universities include:

— A demonstration of commitment from senior executive: Full, visible and tangible support from senior university executives is critical to success in implementing sustainability strategies. A clear signal can be sent to the university community by becoming a signatory to one of the key declarations on sustainability in higher education.

— A 'triple-bottom line' perspective: sustainable universities focus not only on efforts to 'green' the curriculum and their management practices but also on measures to promote social and economic sustainability.

— A sustainability strategy: universities that are successful tend to have a comprehensive strategy for sustainability that has been negotiated and agreed through the university's decision-making structures.

— Implementation and cultural change: the likelihood of sustainability strategies leading to real outcomes depends on successful cultural change across a university, and developing appropriate attitudes and skills among students and administrative and academic staff.

— Monitoring and evaluation: a process for regular monitoring and evaluation and reporting is vital to ensuring continuous and effective implementation.

## Traning for Teachers of the 21st century

Around the world, there are over about 60 million teachers in the world, and every one is potentially a key agent for bringing about the changes in values and lifestyles needed for sustainable development. Consequently, innovative teacher education is needed to tap this potential. Indeed, this was a key priority within Chapter 36 of Agenda 21 and associated Work Programmes developed for education. The administrations and faculties of institutions of teacher education have the potential to bring about tremendous change, because they create the teacher education curriculum, train new teachers, provide professional development for practicing teachers, consult with local schools, and often provide expert opinion to regional and national ministries of education.

Key initiatives around the world to promote teacher education for sustainability over the past decade include:

— a Toolbox in-service education project conducted by the National Consortium for Environmental Education and Training in the United States

— diverse initiatives in the United Kingdom sponsored by WWF, Forum for the Future and the UK Panel on Sustainable Development and several local education authorities

— the Environmental Education Initiative in Teacher Education in Europe

— the UNESCO Learning for a Sustainable Environment: Innovation in Teacher Education project in Asia and the Pacific

— a professional development programme for over 70 teacher education colleges in the province of Karnataka in India

— a network of teacher education and resource centres in China sponsored by WWF

— a national teacher education programme in New Zealand that has trained over 40 people to provide in-service training for teachers in their local regions

— a national teacher education programme in South Africa that has appointed a coordinator in each province, established a range of curriculum and resource development projects, and is developing a national structure for the accreditation of teachers who complete the courses

— an international network of some 50 teacher education institutions, each of which is conducting a project to reorient all or part of its pre-service curriculum towards sustainability, facilitated by a UNESCO Chair for the Reorientation of Teacher Training to Address Sustainability at York University (Canada)

— the on-line and CD-ROM based multimedia teacher education programme, Teaching and Learning for a Sustainable Future, developed by UNESCO as a demonstration project for adaptation and translation to suit local educational and cultural contexts.

The challenge of sustainable development is difficult and complex and, poses particular challenges to education planners, institutions, and teachers. Chief among these is achieving an understanding of the meaning of sustainable development appropriate for educational settings. However, this problem is not really that difficult

—at its heart is the simple idea of ensuring a better quality of life for everyone, now and for generations to come, and this is the entire purpose of education in a nutshell.

Sustainable development simply provides a framework for thinking about what sort of world this could be, and what is needed to build such a world, that is, what goals, values, concepts and skills will be needed. Analysis of lessons learnt over the past decade of educational innovation illustrates that educational systems and institutions are coming to understand the importance of education for sustainable development, the new vision of education it encompasses, and the contributions it can make to basic education, secondary, technical and vocational and higher education, in teacher education and in adult and community education.

While progress has been significant, it has been uneven. No one country displays all the possible dimensions of education for sustainable development and no country has integrated education into all aspects of its sustainable development plan. Among the significant remaining issues and challenges are the following:

— better integrating education for sustainable development into sustainable development policies in a wider range of countries, e.g. economic, environment and population policies

— better integrating education for sustainable development as a framework for education policies, especially national action plans related to EFA goals

— developing and implementing policies, guidelines and strategic plans on education for sustainable development more widely

- — addressing issues of governance to improve coordination between Ministries of Education and Ministries of Environment, Natural Resources, Agriculture, etc.
- — emphasising education for sustainable development in non-formal education as well as in formal education
- — strengthening institutional capacity building and professional development processes for improved planning and implementation of education for sustainable development
- — increasing monitoring, evaluation and reporting of sustainable development education initiatives and their outcomes and impacts
- — increasing attention to the sustainability of initiatives so that policies, programmes and activities are embedded in long-term education plans and financial arrangements.

For a the sustainable future of the world there is the need to make education more inclusive, to enrol all children in schools or alternative programmes and provide adolescents and adults with opportunities for initial and continuing learning. Such strategies should emphasise the inclusion of women and girls, who are so often excluded, because educating girls and women has major benefits, not only in terms of reducing the numbers of children and improving their health and wellbeing, but also because women make up half the world's workforce and their deep concerns with quality of life issues makes gender a prime sustainable development issue. Improving the orientation and quality of existing programmes is another prime need. An existing secondary curriculum, for example, can be oriented towards sustainability by re-thinking the ends it serves and adjusting its content and approach to suit the new objectives being pursued. Such reforms, whether to secondary education or higher education, can yield significant results without requiring huge efforts or imposing enormous expenditures. Population education, health education, education for sustainable consumption, appropriate vocational education – all need to be integrated into core learning for people of all ages.

# Bibliography


B.D. Bhatt, *Curriculum Reform: Change and Continuity*, New Delhi, Kanishka, 1996.

Bhawna Misra, *Current Issues in Modern Education*, New Delhi, Mohit Pub., 2002.

Brooks, Gary D. & Burns, Richard W. (eds.) 1970. *Curriculum Design in a Changing Society*. NJ: Educational Technology Publications.

Cawelti, Gordon, 1974. *Vitalizing the High School: A curriculum critique of major reform proposals*. Association for Supervision and Curriculum Development, 1701 K Street, N.W. Suite 1100, Washington, D.C..

Cay, Donald F. 1966. *Curriculum: Design for Learning*. NY: Bobbs-Merrill Company, Inc.

Gagn, R., 1985. *The conditions of learning*. New York: Holt, Rinehart, and Winston.

H.P. Dikshit, Suresh Garg, Santosh Panda and Vijayshri, (ed.), *Access and Equity : Challenges for Open and Distance Learning*, New Delhi, Kogan Page India, 2002.

Knox, Richard A. 1995. BrainChild. *The Boston Globe Magazine*. November 5th edition. Globe Newspaper Co, P.O. Box 2378, Boston.

P. Renga Ramanujam, *Distance Open Learning: Challenges to Developing Countries*, Delhi, Shipra, 2002.

Postman, Neil, 1995. Virtual Students, Digital Classroom. *The Nation*. October 9th edition. The Nation Company, L.P., 72 Fifth Avenue, NY 10011.

Sameer Pralhad Narkhede, *Challenges of Higher Education in India*, New Delhi, Sarup, 2001.

Straker, Anna 1989. *Children Using Computers*. Oxford, UK: Basil Blackwell Ltd.

Thompson, James, 1994. Systemic Education Reform. *Eric Digest*. No. 90.

V.D. Madan, *Higher Education Beyond 2000: An Omni-Tech Approach*, New Delhi, Kanishka, 2002.

W.G. Reeder, *Introduction to Education*, New Delhi, Mohit, 2001.

Yazali Josephine, (ed.), *International Conference on Globalisation and Challenges for Education* : Focus on Equity and Equality, Delhi, Shipra, 2003.

# Index